ADVANCE PRAISE FOR

W. B. Yeats and the Upaniṣads

"Yeats's absorption in Upanisadic thought is a subject that criticism has hitherto skirted, or treated warily. Here, for the first time, is an exploration by an author who combines a deep immersion in the subject with a rich understanding of Yeats's development as a poet and a thinker. Shalini Sikka examines and explains the reasons for Yeats's turning to the Upaniṣads where he found 'an ancient discipline, a philosophy that satisfied the intellect' (Yeats). Written with grace and lucidity and based on impeccable scholarship, this book is a must buy for any Yeats aficionado."

R. W. Desai, Former Professor of English, University of Delhi;
Author, Yeats's Shakespeare; *Editor,* Hamlet Studies

"Yeats realized through his study of the Upaniṣads that knowledge and wisdom are both indispensable for the healthy conduct of life. While knowledge of the arts and sciences is necessary for life in the worldly/social spheres, a dilution of the ego is essential for preparing the mind for communion with the spiritual hierarchy; the dawn of wisdom solves riddles which cannot be tackled through mundane know-how. The presence of these ideas in Yeats's writings is the subject of Shalini Sikka's book."

B. R. Sharma, Professor of Sanskrit, University of Delhi;
Author, The Concept of Ātman in the Principal Upaniṣads

"Shalini Sikka's well-researched book explores many new sites wherein Yeats's thought intriguingly relates to the thought of the Upaniṣads. New light is thrown, among other things, on Yeats's view of the imagination, his concept of Unity of Being, and on the bewildering symbolism of *A Vision.*"

G. K. Das, Former Professor of English, University of Delhi;
Vice-Chancellor, Utkal University, Bhubaneswar, Orissa

W. B. Yeats
and the Upaniṣads

Irish Studies

Robert Mahony
General Editor

Vol. 6

PETER LANG
New York • Washington, D.C./Baltimore • Bern
Frankfurt am Main • Berlin • Brussels • Vienna • Oxford

Shalini Sikka

W. B. Yeats and the Upaniṣads

PETER LANG
New York • Washington, D.C./Baltimore • Bern
Frankfurt am Main • Berlin • Brussels • Vienna • Oxford

Library of Congress Cataloging-in-Publication Data

Sikka, Shalini.
W. B. Yeats and the Upaniṣads / Shalini Sikka.
p. cm. — (Irish studies; vol. 6)
Includes bibliographical references and index.
1. Yeats, W. B. (William Butler), 1865–1939—Knowledge—India.
2. Yeats, W. B. (William Butler), 1865–1939—Philosophy. 3. English poetry—Irish authors—Indic influences. 4. Philosophy, Indic, in literature.
5. Hinduism in literature. 6. India—In literature. 7. Upanishads.
I. Title. II. Irish studies (New York, N.Y.); vol. 6.
PR5908.I48 S55 821'.8—dc21 99-058127
ISBN 0-8204-4926-1
ISSN 1043-5743

Die Deutsche Bibliothek-CIP-Einheitsaufnahme

Sikka, Shalini:
W. B. Yeats and the Upaniṣads / Shalini Sikka.
–New York; Washington, D.C./Baltimore; Bern;
Frankfurt am Main; Berlin; Brussels; Vienna; Oxford: Lang.
(Irish studies; Vol. 6)
ISBN 0-8204-4926-1

The paper in this book meets the guidelines for permanence and durability of the Committee on Production Guidelines for Book Longevity of the Council of Library Resources.

Printed in the United States of America

To my parents

Janki Anand
and
Indranath Anand

Table of Contents

Acknowledgments

I wish to express my deeply felt gratitude to several people, without whose guidance and help a book on Yeats and the Upaniṣads, an area both vast and abstruse, could not have been written. Professor G.K. Das, with unerring critical acumen, helped me in selecting the areas to be worked upon, and gave me the benefit of his scholarly advice from time to time. To him I am deeply indebted. My special thanks are due to Professor R.W. Desai, a Yeats scholar at the University of Delhi, who gave me the benefit of his erudition throughout. His suggestions and insightful comments enabled me to fortify many an argument in this work. Professor B.R. Sharma, a renowned scholar of the Upaniṣads and Indian spiritual lore helped deepen my knowledge of the subject. I gratefully acknowledge the encouragement and inspiration received from him in traversing the difficult terrain of the Upaniṣads. Dr. John Kelly, whom I met in Oxford at an early stage in the project, shared my enthusiasm; he lent me copies of unpublished letters of Yeats to Shree Purohit Swāmi, Shri Hamsa, and George Russell—I am indebted to him. I have great pleasure in recording Anne Yeats's graciousness and hospitality in allowing me to consult books in her father's library in her picturesque house in Dalkey, near Dublin. I wish to thank my series editor Robert Mahony for his guidance in giving final shape to this book. I owe thanks also to my father Shri Indra Nath Anand who introduced me to the Upaniṣads in the first place, and endorsed my plan to write this book.

I am thankful to my husband Pawan, children Saurabh and Ayushi (grown up since this work began!) for their infinite patience as well as support throughout the project. I also wish to thank Vatsala Khurana, my friend and colleague, for a warm and rare friendship that kept my spirits up throughout. I appreciate the help received from my son Saurabh in searching for a suitable type-face; he downloaded the Tamal font from www.chakra.org, without which the transliteration of Sanskrit words would have been impossible.

For permission to reprint extracts from Yeats's works, listed below, grateful acknowledgment is made to A.P. Watt Ltd. on behalf of Michael B. Yeats, and to Scribner, a Division of Simon and Schuster: from *A Vision* by W.B. Yeats (copyright 1937 by W.B. Yeats; copyright renewed © 1965 by Bertha Georgie Yeats and Anne Butler Yeats); from *Essays and Introductions* by W.B. Yeats (copyright © 1961 by Mrs. W.B. Yeats); from *Explorations* by W.B. Yeats (copyright © 1962 by Mrs. W.B. Yeats); from *The Collected Poems of W.B. Yeats* (Revised Second Edition) edited by Richard J. Finneran (copyright 1924, 1928, 1933, 1934 by Macmillan Publishing Company; copyrights renewed © 1952, 1961, 1962 by Bertha Georgie Yeats, and 1956 by Georgie Yeats; copyright 1940 by Georgie Yeats; copyright renewed 1968 by Bertha Georgie Yeats, Michael Butler Yeats, and Anne Yeats); from *Collected Plays* by W.B. Yeats (copyright 1934, 1952 by Macmillan Publishing Company, renewed 1962 by Bertha Georgie Yeats, and 1980 by Anne Yeats). I am grateful to Michael Yeats for permission to quote from *The Letters of W.B. Yeats* (London: Rupert Hart-Davis, copyright 1953 Michael Yeats). I wish to express my thanks to S. Gopal of the Radhakrishnan Trust for granting permission to reprint quotations from S. Radhakrishnan, *Indian Philosophy* (London: George Allen and Unwin Ltd., 1923), and from S. Radhakrishnan, *The Principal Upaniṣads* (London: George Allen and Unwin Ltd., 1953). All rights reserved. Extracts from Shree Purohit Swāmi, *An Indian Monk, His Life and Adventures* (London: Macmillan, 1932); Shree Purohit Swāmi, trans. *The Holy Mountain* (London: Faber and Faber, 1934); Shree Purohit Swāmi and W.B. Yeats, trans. *The Ten Principal Upanishads* (London: Faber and Faber, 1937); and Shree Purohit Swāmi, trans. *Bhagwān Shri Patanjali: Aphorisms of Yoga* (London: Faber and Faber, 1938) are reprinted by permission of Shree Purohit Swāmi Memorial Trust, Pune 411004. I gratefully acknowledge the permission granted by S. Praṣad on behalf of the trustees of the Shree Purohit Swāmi Memorial Trust to quote from the unpublished talk given by Shree Purohit Swāmi at Madras University in 1938. I owe thanks to Russell E.

Murphy, editor, *Yeats Eliot Review* for granting me permission to reprint extracts from my articles: 'W.B. Yeats and the Upaniṣads: An Introductory Note' (Vol. XII, 2, 1993); 'Yeats's concept of Unity of Being in the Light of the Upanisadic States of Turīya and Suṣupti' (Vol. XII, 3-4, 1994). All rights reserved.

The cooperation and help received from librarians at the following institutions is gratefully acknowledged: Bodleian Library, Oxford; National Library of Ireland, Dublin; The Theosophical Society in England, London; Theosophical Library and Research Centre, Adyar, Madras; Central Reference Library, University of Delhi, Delhi; Nehru Museum and Library, New Delhi; Annie Besant Theosophical Library, Delhi; British Council Library, New Delhi; Jesus and Mary College Library, New Delhi.

Shalini Sikka
New Delhi, November 2001.

Introduction

W.B. Yeats's fascination with esoteric disciplines in general, and his interest in India and its ancient wisdom remains a largely unexplored area for Yeats scholars, over six decades after he passed away. The first phase of Yeatsian criticism acknowledged the greatness of Yeats's poetry while regretting the presence in it of obscure occult doctrines. This trend seemed to have been started by Yeats's own friend and adviser, W.T. Horton, who disapproved of Yeats's obsession with spirits and automatic writing. Even though George Mills Harper has called theirs "an occult friendship," Horton wrote to Yeats in 1914, that it almost disgusted him to see Yeats's sitting on the floor and searching for an automatic script among his papers, while his guests sat around him.[1] Horton complained that poetry ought to have been his only concern. Critics who came soon after Yeats's day echoed this mood.

W.H. Auden felt that Yeats was occupied with the "mumbo jumbo of magic and the nonsense of India," and that he made it the "centre of his work"; Cleanth Brooks (1939) voiced his disapproval from a scientific platform and found Yeats's gyres, his "frank acceptance of the supernatural, enough to try the patience of any scientific modernist." R.P. Blackmur, writing in 1936 had considered the difficulty of accepting the supernatural, which, according to him, was "not part of our mental furniture" and could be dismissed as "debris to be swept away."[2]

In fact Auden's shadow was long enough to stretch into the eighties. Graham Hough, in *The Mystery Religion of W.B. Yeats* (1984), wrote that there was, surrounding Yeats, "a riotous profusion of prescriptions, magic formulas, rituals and symbolic texts, incubated in the carefully protected hothouses of hidden cults."[3] In 1984, Elizabeth Cullingford, introducing the critical anthology, *Yeats:*

Poems 1919-1935, largely endorsed Allen Tate, who had said in 1942 that while Yeats's esoteric symbolism would be understood by scholars, a study of the poetry itself would be postponed. She acknowledged that Yeats's magical theories in prose might throw some light on the meaning of his poetry, but argued that for all the hard work this would involve, ultimately it would only be a substitute for a study of the poetry proper. According to her, studies or records of Yeats's occult practices, difficult although interesting are "recommended for hard core enthusiasts only"; the works she mentioned were *Yeats's Golden Dawn* (1974) by George Mills Harper, and Harper's edition of a critical anthology, *Yeats and the Occult* (1976).[4]

Such thinking may have created the mindset which made Western criticism steer clear of Indian thought in the work of Yeats. Yeats anticipated, as well as answered this kind of criticism, but his statements have not been taken entirely seriously. The arbitrary and summary dismissal by modernist thought of the metaphysical and the supernatural would, one feels, call forth the same response from Yeats as the one he gave regarding Locke. When Locke did not and could not explain the skill shown by a bird in making its nest, as he was not aware of "innate ideas" or anima mundi, his logic ("I did not write to explain the actions of dumb creatures"), according to Yeats, is endorsed by modern enlightenment, but perhaps modern enlightenment is itself under a hypnosis and is "not free to think otherwise." Yeats felt that ignoring the metaphysical, the supernatural, or for that matter, any significant part of human experience leads us to findings that are incomplete and therefore invalid: "how trust historian and psychologist that have for three hundred years ignored in writing of the history of the world, or of the human mind, so momentous a part of human experience? What else had they ignored and distorted?"[5]

Apart from the fact that it is not warranted to ignore these fundamental pronouncements of the poet regarding his basic convictions, it must be noted that these words of Yeats form a fitting context in which to study his interest in India. It is well known that Yeats formed friendships with enlightened Indians like Mohini Chatterjee, Tagore, and Purohit Swāmi, as well as with Western devotees of Indian thought like George Russell (AE), Charles

Johnston, and Madame Blavatsky. It is also well known that Yeats wrote introductions to Tagore's *Gitanjali* (1912) of which he spoke in glowing terms, to Purohit Swāmi's autobiography, *An Indian Monk* (1932), to Bhagwān Shri Hamsa's *The Holy Mountain* (1934), and to Patanjali's *Aphorisms of Yoga* (1938).[6] An important fact in this connection is Yeats's decision to spend some time in Majorca with Purohit Swāmi, assisting him in the task of preparing an English translation of the Upaniṣads,[7] which was then published as *The Ten Principal Upanishads* (1937).[8] To this work Yeats wrote a Preface, a careful reading of which would give scholars an insight not only into the relevance of the Upaniṣads to Europe, but also into certain fundamental preoccupations of Yeats as a poet.

However, a few studies have thrown light on this aspect of the poet's interest. While discussing Madame Blavatsky and the impact of her ideas on Yeats quite early in life, Richard Ellmann in *Yeats: The Man and the Masks* (1948), made known the key fact that there were connections between *A Vision* (1925) and Theosophy[9]—a point, however, that has not been adequately explored. Indian scholars have produced studies dealing with this aspect of Yeats, among them H.R. Bachchan's *W.B. Yeats and Occultism* (1959),[10] and Narayan Hegde's unpublished thesis, "W.B. Yeats and Purohit Swāmi: A Study of Yeats's Last Indian Phase" (1980).[11] Bachchan examined Yeats's relationship with Mohini Chatterjee in the light of Śaṁkara's philosophy of regarding the world and all action in it as illusory. In a chapter on 'Purohit Swāmi and *The Upanishads*,' Bachchan discussed some parallels between Yeats's later work and the Upaniṣads as studied by Yeats under the guidance of Purohit Swāmi. Narayan Hegde dealt chiefly with the personalities of Purohit Swāmi and Bhagwān Shri Hamsa in the Bhakti Yoga tradition. He also drew significant parallels between the Upaniṣads and the later poems and plays of Yeats; significantly, he maintained that the ideas expressed in the first version of *A Vision* embodied several aspects of Indian thought that Yeats had learnt through theosophy.

However, the findings of these critics and the groundwork they prepared, have not been incorporated into the business of practical criticism and analysis of his poetry. It is apparent that most Western critics have regarded Yeats's interest in Western myths, symbols, and iconography on the one hand, and his interest in Eastern thought on the other, as mutually exclusive areas. Elizabeth Cullingford in her introduction to the critical anthology, *Yeats: Poems 1919-1935,* while discussing the task of approaching Yeats's poetry through his debts, mentions Blake, Shelley, Ben Jonson, Plato and others but completely overlooks the Upaniṣads and the *Bhagavad-Gītā* in her list.[12] Graham Hough, in *The Mystery Religion of W.B. Yeats*, takes the view that "obscure, puzzling and apparently original elements in Yeats's esoteric doctrine...have their roots in the Theosophical teaching he first encountered in his early twenties." He frowns upon Yeats's association with Madame Blavatsky, whom the Society for Psychical Research had declared to be a fraud; she was "bad company" that Yeats was compelled to keep, as she was able to reveal "the hidden channels of human experience."[13] It must be affirmed here that Yeats penetrated beyond the idiosyncrasies of Madame Blavatsky, and as I have shown in this book, had an unerring instinct for absorbing the essentials of her teaching and the teachings of Theosophy.

Kathleen Raine in *Yeats the Initiate* (1986) is the first perhaps of Western critics who notes that "many critics, including some whose motive is to 'protect' Yeats's reputation have continued to scoff."[14] In her lecture 'Yeats and Kabir,' delivered to the Yeats Society in New Delhi, in 1983, she had cleared the ground for studies in this direction: "Of all modern Western poets the one to have been most deeply and continuously influenced by India is the greatest of all—William Butler Yeats."[15] Like Ellmann and Bachchan earlier, she reiterated the Indian connections of Theosophy: "In however confused a form, The Theosophical Society did bring the metaphysical thought of India" to the West. In 'Hades Wrapped in Cloud,' Raine had already spoken of the need of Yeats's critics to read "the Indian and Far Eastern scriptures," that were being read by the Theosophists at the turn of the century.[16]

However, George Mills Harper in *Yeats's Golden Dawn*, as well as Kathleen Raine think that Yeats turned away from the "eastern-oriented" Theosophical Society to the western esotericism of the Order of the Golden Dawn.[17] Actually, Yeats was asked to resign, as he was a supporter of evocation of spirits, an aspect of occult experimentation disallowed by the Theosophical Society.[18] As a practical occultist Yeats was interested not so much in Eastern or Western tradition at this early stage as in the truth underlying occult phenomena. Even in the Golden Dawn, the unity underlying both traditions was emphasized. In a lecture to the members of the Golden Dawn, Westcott had stated that the Eastern school of Theosophy and the Hermetic Society of the Golden Dawn were "fraternities of students whose predecessors must have come from the same stock of *Magi*...."[19] Also, Mohini Chatterjee lectured to both the Societies. The real criticism of Yeats against the Theosophical Society was that it was too theoretical, and "by teaching an abstract system without experiment or evidence they were making their pupils dogmatic...."[20] He recorded in his *Memoirs* that the rituals of the Golden Dawn inspired him to form plans for deeds of all kinds, whereas after attending meetings of the Esoteric Section, he " had no desire but for more thought, more discussion."[21] Yeats, however, brought away with him intense conviction of certain Upanisadic truths as professed by Madame Blavatsky. This explains his impassioned plea for unity in his essay, 'Is the Order of R.R. and A.C. to remain a Magical Order?'[22] Harper has pointed out that the members of the latter Society did not understand some of his convictions. Yeats had already admitted the "inherent weight of the philosophy"[23] of theosophy, and in practical occultism offered by the Golden Dawn, was seeking a confirmation of the theories he understood. The Upanisadic background of Yeats's view is here discussed in the chapter entitled, "Imagination," What the Upaniṣads Have Named "Self."

To dispel the fear of critics that a study of Yeats's magical theories threatens to become "a substitute for the study of poetry proper," it must be stated that although, normally, the assumptions of spiritual practice are different from those made by literary criticism, Yeats stands firmly in the penumbra where the two overlap. As Kathleen Raine has stated very succinctly, "Yeats was a metaphysician for whom poetry was the language of spiritual knowledge." The fundamental problem is that the student of esoteric knowledge (whether belonging to Cabala, Gnosticism, or Hinduism, as they all share some common ground), would obtain an instantaneous insight into some of Yeats's words (whether spoken as magician or poet), yet it rarely happens that such a practitioner strays into the realm of literary criticism.

A fall-out of ignoring Yeats's interest in Eastern wisdom has been the tendency to regard Yeats as so subjective as to be almost idiosyncratic. For instance, Harold Bloom had warned that "the

Higher Criticism of Yeats, when it is more fully developed, will have to engage the radical issue of his subjectivity...."[24] Thomas Parkinson had also noticed that there is "increasing individuation of thought in Yeats."[25]

To Yeats, poetry and the search for fundamental truths were parallel preoccupations. His early experiments with evocation of thought or emotion through symbols, opened up interesting areas of speculation: "a man walked, as it were, casting a shadow, and yet one could never say which was man and which was shadow." The question he considered was: how far civilization, politics or any set of observable facts were the result of thought and emotions—in other words, how judge the objective world when there was evidence that it may be the creation of subjective impulses? To this fundamental question were linked other, more practical questions:

> How could I judge any scheme of education, or of social reform, when I could not measure what the different classes and occupations contributed to that invisible commerce of reverie and of sleep; and what is luxury and what necessity when a fragment of gold braid or a flower in the wall paper may be an originating impulse to revolution or to philosophy?[26]

To him, it seemed that modern enlightenment did not have the answers, as it chose to dismiss or ignore certain aspects of human experience that it was not equipped to explain. Therefore, Yeats felt, it was important to study the mind and its powers before addressing social questions. It was for this reason that English literature "cast off its preoccupation with social problems and began to...ask the most profound questions," explained Yeats in his Preface to *The Ten Principal Upanishads*. This and related ideas led him to trace any philosophical idea that interested him to its earliest use, and made him believe that there must be a tradition of belief older and more comprehensive than any European Church. However, in his studies of Irish folklore, in Lady Gregory's *Visions and Beliefs*, he found something of what he wanted but not all; he felt that "the explanatory intellect had disappeared."[27]

In the Upaniṣads and in Purohit Swāmi's spiritual journey, *An Indian Monk*, he found what he was seeking, "an ancient discipline, a philosophy that satisfied the intellect." As noted earlier, it is not as though the Upaniṣads were texts that he encountered towards the close of his life. The ideas of the Upaniṣads had been available to him through theosophy, his association with Mohini Chatterjee, George Russell, and Charles Johnston, in the work of Tagore, Max-Mueller and R.E. Hume. In fact, when Mohini Chatterjee spoke of consciousness to the members of the London Lodge of The Theosophical Society, he was presenting an Upanisadic idea; Yeats recorded that "it was his first meeting with a philosophy that confirmed his vague speculations and seemed at once logical and boundless."[28]

In his Preface to *The Ten Principal Upanishads*, Yeats stated that in the Upaniṣads every fundamental problem of philosophy had been touched upon, while at the same time, the Upaniṣads were "compositions, not writings, for they were sung..."[29]

It now remains to outline briefly the gradual process through which Yeats was attracted to the Upaniṣads, and the areas wherein they complemented his thought. The Upaniṣads are philosophical and religious texts whose aim is the direct mystical experience of reality. The word *upaniṣad* is composed of *upa* (near), *ni* (down), and *sad* (to sit), and means "sitting down near." Pupils who had gone through a special preliminary training and given proof of their fitness, sat in close rapport with the teacher who imparted the mysteries of the universe to them. *Upaniṣad* also means the secret, or the esoteric doctrine. *The Svetāśvatara Upaniṣad* refers to "the highest mystic doctrine" as *upaniṣad* from the root *sad*, "to loosen" or "to destroy"; this derivation indicates that it is through *Brahma Vidya* or the knowledge of the Absolute that ignorance is "loosened" or destroyed. The Upaniṣads are the concluding portions of the Vedas, so their philosophy is also referred to as the Vedānta. The principal Upaniṣads belong to the eighth and seventh centuries B.C. and are pre-Buddhistic.

Yeats outlined some of his fundamental aims as a poet from time to time. As a young man he stated with great surety, that his wish was "to discover and communicate a state of being."[30] Another basic conviction of his was that a poet must rediscover and restate traditional wisdom, and that none but "that stroke of luckless luck can open before him the accumulated experience of the world". He recorded in *Autobiographies* that there must be "a tradition of belief older than any European Church and founded upon the experience of the world before the modern bias." The two aims were really inter-related. At the core of great art was a state of ecstasy; this was enshrined in traditional wisdom where the poet must seek it. He said:

> Supreme art is a traditional statement of certain heroic and religious truths, passed on from age to age, modified by individual genius, but never abandoned.[31]

The Upaniṣads came to be among Yeats's sources for the much sought ancient wisdom.[32] Mohini Chatterjee's lecture to the London Lodge of The Theosophical Society in December 1884, "On the Higher Aspect of Theosophic Studies," was a compact presentation of Upanisadic philosophy, although the word "Upaniṣad" was used only once.[33] Yeats was fascinated, as he seemed to have found something strangely familiar in this apparently alien thought, and recorded that he found a philosophy that "confirmed his vague speculations and seemed at once logical and boundless." Yeats recalled that in 1886 or a little later he lived at The Theosophical Society, Upper Ely Place where he first took an interest in the Upaniṣads.[34] Yeats's interest in the Upaniṣads was also nurtured by his friend AE (George Russell), poet and mystic as well as a student of ancient Indian wisdom. Later, Yeats would record that for some forty years his friend had quoted passages from some Upaniṣad.[35]

Yeats became aware that the Upaniṣads were a body of texts that contained preoccupations and thoughts that were akin to his own. Subjecting his own and contemporary poetry to scrutiny, and discovering the reasons for its decadence was a step in that direction. He found that "when a man puts only his contemplative nature and his more vague desires into his art, the sensuous images through which it speaks become broken, fleeting, uncertain, or are chosen for their distance from general experience, and all grows unsubstantial and fantastic."[36] He discovered that decadence resulted when a poet created only from one part of his mind, from a fraction of his total experience. The other cause of weakness of his early plays and poems was the predominance in them of abstraction and philosophy that had not been transmuted into art. His wish was to possess an imagination like that of Chaucer's, one that expressed itself in terms of character and action rather than abstractions.[37]

His experiments with evocation through symbols revealed to him a deeper level of consciousness, resulting in turn in mature poetic practices. The discovery of *anima mundi* made possible poems like

'The Second Coming' and 'A Prayer for My Daughter.' Yeats was now transformed from a decadent poet who composed verse expressing merely his personal desires, into one who could "see" images in the memory of the race, a poet-sage who spoke on behalf of the one mind. He spoke of bringing his mind close to the mind of Indian and Japanese poets, lay brothers in medieval monasteries and learned authors who derived their authority from tradition, in order to enter the mind that was called "the subconscious."[38] As these words show, Yeats was seeking a state that lay beyond the racial mind, the universal or the "general mind," a clear indication that notwithstanding the progressive complexity and maturity of his poetry, he had not lost sight of the aforementioned early aim to discover and communicate a specific state of mind.

His letters to Sturge Moore indicate that he was sifting through Western and Eastern philosophies to find a system of thought that was most suited to his needs as a poet, a system that would bestow philosophic sanction on his experiences and preoccupations, and also deliver him from abstraction. He finally accepted Vedantic thought as being closest to his own poetic theory and practice. Of Vedantic thought he said: "this seems to me the simplest and to liberate us from all manner of abstraction and create at once a joyous, artistic life."[39] Yeats's study of the Upaniṣads was also of help to him in interpreting the thought of *A Vision*. He admitted that the tradition of Western thought did not entirely help him to understand the revelations of his instructors. Presenting the revised version, he wrote that apart from two or three of the principal Platonic Dialogues he knew no philosophy, and admitted that Blake, Swedenborg, Boehme or the Cabala could not help him.[40] However, Yeats had encountered in theosophy some of the thought of the Upaniṣads presented directly or indirectly and much of it, along with similar material he found elsewhere, had sunk into his subconscious mind and largely formed the subject matter of *A Vision* (1925).[41] As mentioned earlier, some critics have noted the connection of theosophy with *A Vision* but not explored its content. Subjecting his own work to scrutiny he found that while there were differences between neo-Platonic philosophy, hermetic fragments, and *A Vision*, there were similarities between his work and Upaniṣadic thought. In order to give lucid expression to this thought Yeats needed to make a conscious and proper study of the Upaniṣads. In 1932, he finished reading R.E. Hume's edition of *The Thirteen Principal Upanishads*. The last page of his copy bears the date "23.1.32" in Yeats's hand; the text has been carefully read and marked, bearing Yeats's comments at many places.[42] It was only after reading Hume's edition of the Upaniṣads that Yeats came across Purohit Swāmi. He wrote to Olivia Shakespear on March 9, 1932, informing her that he had "a long manuscript by an Indian saint to read—the wonderful thing I told you of: the reality of which the theosophists have dreamed."[43]

Yeats's trip to Majorca with Purohit Swāmi in 1935 gave him the threefold advantage of mastering the philosophy of the Upaniṣads, of helping in their translation into contemporary English, and of enriching his imagination. Purohit Swāmi wrote to Yeats just before the trip: "I am longing to be with you and to have the proud privilege of discussing the Upanishads."[44] It is evident that the Swāmi elucidated some points that may not have been clear to Yeats from his reading of Hume's edition. He wrote to Olivia Shakespear, "I have learnt a good deal from the Swāmi who suddenly makes all wisdom if you ask him the right questions."[45] In Vedānta and the Upaniṣads Yeats found corroboration as well as a finer definition of some of his basic beliefs and preoccupations. They offered examples of supreme poetry as well as high philosophy, as Yeats noted in his Preface to *The Ten Principal Upanishads*. The major themes touched upon by the Upaniṣads are the creation of the cosmos, the human condition subject to nescience or *avidyā*, resulting in *karma* and cyclic reincarnation, self-realization and release from bondage, and the attainment of a supreme, blissful state of consciousness as the final aim of human existence. These are inter-related themes and at different periods in his life Yeats was interested in one or several simultaneously, as a scrutiny of his works reveals.

Yeats assisted the Swāmi in rendering the Sanskrit scriptures into modern English. In the first chapter, "*The Ten Principal Upanishads:* Some Aspects of the Translation by Yeats and Purohit Swāmi," I have examined some of the features of this work. The Yeats-Swāmi edition is more accessible to the modern western reader (in comparison to R.E. Hume's and Radhakrishnan's translations), as here the translators avoid references to mythological figures and esoteric ceremonies that would require to be glossed; wherever needed Yeats substituted western symbols for eastern ones in order to achieve greater intelligibility. Yeats made some useful suggestions to Purohit Swāmi regarding the work of translation: he wrote to Ethel Mannin that the Swāmi was astonished to discover that he could "call a goddess 'this handsome girl,' or even 'a pretty girl,' instead of a 'maiden of surpassing loveliness.'"[46] There was also a creative dimension to Yeats's project; he wrote to Olivia Shakespear of his wish to work on the Upaniṣads in order to be "reborn in imagination."[47] Interestingly, while on the one hand the translation bears a definitely Yeatsian stamp, on the other, an interfusion seems to have taken place between Yeats's thought and that of the Upaniṣads.

Another problem that surfaces in Yeatsian criticism is understanding *A Vision* (1937) itself or using it to explain certain poems with its help, without going into the Upanisadic doctrines underlying it. Yeats worked simultaneously on revising *A Vision* and helping Purohit Swāmi in translating *The Ten Principal Upanishads*. On 15 May 1937, Yeats wrote to the Swāmi: "Before the end of summer *A Vision* will be out and only in India can I find anybody who can throw light upon certain of its problems."[48] In this context, only Ellmann has pointed out that the twenty-eight phase lunar cycle is reminiscent of "the Dark Fortnight and Bright Fortnight of Brahminism."[49] Actually, Yeats himself said that this symbolism was not found by him in any classical author, but in the Upaniṣads, and added, "the conflict of light and dark...concerned him most."[50] Summing up Madame Blavatsky's view of creation as a "periodical and consecutive appearance of the universe from the subjective on to the objective plane of being, at regular intervals of time," Graham Hough comments that there are endless philosophical difficulties in conceiving such a process. He then goes on to explain it in terms of the Cabala, where there are "a series of emanations, each giving rise to the next...till in the end we arrive at the material world...."[51] This problem I have discussed at length in the second chapter, "Yeats's View of Nature in the Light of the Upaniṣads" where I point out that in *A Vision* (1925), Yeats had been uncertain whether his instructors were offering an idealist or evolutionist explanation of creation. Yeats was enabled to arrive at his answer by his study of the Upaniṣads, and in the revised version of *A Vision*, made Robartes his spokesman for the idealist theory while repudiating the cabalist view: "Life is no series of emanations from divine reason such as the Cabalists imagine...."[52]

The Upaniṣads brought him to a closer understanding of the question of ultimate reality. He noted in the first version of *A Vision* that he had not really considered it, nor had his documents thrown any light upon it.[53] Two of his early works, the short story, 'Where there is Nothing, there is God,' and the play *The Unicorn From the Stars* indicate that he was interested in the theme. But he was directly confronted with the question of ultimate reality when he was seeking sources in Plotinus for some revelations of his instructors: "In Plotinus the one is the good, whereas in the system good and evil are eliminated before the soul can be united to Reality, being that stream of phenomena that drowns us."[54] However, the "nothing" that he had spoken of in his early works emerged as the symbol of the "sphere" in the automatic script, and it would take Yeats much familiarity with Upanisadic thought before he understood it entirely. "Nothing," or *asat*, was at the base of the manifested reality, or nature. In Yeats's system reality is analysed into the *Four Principles*: *Husk, Passionate Body, Spirit*, and *Celestial Body*. These appear as the *Four Faculties* of man: *Will, Mask, Creative Mind,* and *Body of Fate*. He understood from his study of the Upaniṣads that these were the four stages of creation as well as the four states of consciousness in the microcosm. The stages of creation as described in the *Ṛg Veda* and the Upaniṣads are: the Absolute, the One or the subject-object complex, the cosmic soul with ideas of creation in their subtle form, and finally, the world. The relationship between the *Principles*, the *Faculties*, and man's changing personality symbolised by the phases of the moon appeared in *A Vision* (both versions), *The Herne's Egg*, and 'Supernatural Songs.'

What is obscurely or inadequately understood by readers of *The Herne's Egg*, for instance, becomes intelligible when it is studied in the light of Upanisadic philosophy. Richard Ellmann has summed up the plot of the play at the level of fable: "The hero of *The Herne's Egg*...deliberately and knowingly commits sacrilege against the Great Herne, by raping his priestess....As a result of the desecration, the hero is doomed to die at a fool's hand, but...he kills himself."[55] But on a deeper level, the play embodies the philosophy and the message of the Upaniṣads. The Herne is the Creator, Attracta, His Creation; Congal, the 'hero' represents the common man. The play illustrates the theme of the *Īśa Upaniṣad* stated in the opening verse:

> (Know that) all this, whatever moves in this moving world, is enveloped by God. Therefore find your enjoyment in renunciation, do not covet what belongs to others.[56]

The desecration of Attracta illustrates man's possessive and acquisitive attitude towards the objects of the world. Yeats exploits the obvious comic ramifications of foolishness, especially towards the close of the play. Congal is ignorant of the great truth of the Upaniṣads; being foolish like a donkey, he must be reborn as one. The concluding statement of the play, "All that trouble and nothing to show for it,/ Nothing but just another donkey," might well be the sad utterance of an Upanisadic sage on seeing the antics of man. Yeats wrote to Dorothy Wellesley that the Swāmi was staying with him, and, "the play is his philosophy in a fable, or mine confirmed by him. Every afternoon I go through his translation of the *Upanishads*."[57]

The next chapter, "Death and Immortality," deals with Yeats's interest in séances where he conducted research into post-mortem states, trying to prove the immortality of the soul. He finally recorded in his *Memoirs* in 1913 that he had proved a spirit's identity in the E R case.[58] The Upaniṣads endorsed his findings; in *A Vision* he wrote that these ancient works were addressed to the Norman girl who yearned for immortality.[59]

In 'Anima Mundi,' he referred to two conditions of the soul that he called the condition of fire and the terrestrial condition. These, he found, were paralleled in the Upanisadic paths of the Gods and the Fathers, also symbolized as the bright and dark fortnights. In the Upaniṣads, he discovered also the laws governing eschatology and rebirth. According to Yeats, *Spirit*, when attached to *Passionate Body*, is a record of all the actions of the being spreading over many lifetimes. In the Upaniṣads, this corresponds to the doctrine of *karma* or effect of actions; in other words, good or evil energies released by man must inexorably return to him and so create his reincarnation amid circumstances that Yeats called *Body of Fate*. This record or *karma*, if evil, results in bondage to others, requiring a process of expiation that may last over several lifetimes. This process brings about suffering and self-realization, but as incarnate life depends on desires, it also ensures a fulfilment of man's deepest desires; Yeats ardently accepted the latter idea.

In the chapter on "Unity of Being," I have considered certain fundamental questions regarding Yeats's evaluation of the East. Was his interest in the East an aberration in an otherwise brilliant poetic career? Was it only periodic, an interest that came to the fore because he could not resist visitors to the West like Mohini Chatterjee, Tagore, and Purohit Swāmi, as and when they happened to arrive? And did he finally reaffirm only Western traditions and dismiss the East, treating it only with necessary courtesy? Discussing 'The Statues,' Kathleen Raine says that "Spirituality is the goal of the East, objective science of the West."[60] Hamlet is seen by her as a type of the West, the Buddha as a type of the East; "Yeats, a man of the West, gives in this poem, due honour to Pythagoras."[61] If Yeats is eulogizing Pythagoras, measurement, and the West, dismissing the Buddha and the East, what then is the position of Cuchulain, the Irish hero, who features in a rhetorical question that seems dismissive of calculation, number, and so on? The answer to this is amply explained in the chapter on "Unity," but suffice it to say here that "gong" and "conch," western and eastern symbols of unity of being transcend any neat and simplistic separation of East and West.

Again, in her essay, 'Death-in-Life and Life-in-Death' in *Yeats the Initiate*, Raine speaks of Yeats's disagreement with "Plato's out and out denial of the value of the lower world..." She remarks: "In this it seems Yeats was more Western than Eastern." Here is the popular Western equation of Eastern with ascetic, world-denying, *maya*, illusory. However, in the Upaniṣads, Supreme reality is not a void. It is truth-consciousness-bliss, referred to as *Sat-Cit-Ānanda* in Sanskrit. *The Bhagavad-Gīta* too, with its doctrine of *Karma-Yoga* (enlightenment through action) does not support the world-as-illusion thesis. Yeats, however, was aware of this when he declared his faith in unity of being as Blake's Imagination and the Self of the Upaniṣads.

Harold Bloom, writing on 'A Dialogue of Self and Soul' refers to *A Vision*'s terminology of the *Four Faculties*. He says that "The Soul (and this is the poem's necessary limitation)...has read *A Vision* carefully" and uses its language: "the is and the ought" and "the Knower and the Known."[62] In fact, what is required is that we read *A Vision* in the light of the Upaniṣads. When duality of desire ("is" and "ought") or of knowledge ("knower" and "known") is resolved, the casting out of "remorse" takes place, the being achieves pure consciousness, and realizing that he is Self or *Ātman*, feels that he is blessed by everything. Such liberation is life-affirming, therefore the Soul's offer of a final escape from rebirth is rejected by the poet.

Parkinson among other critics has quoted Yeats: "Man can embody truth but he cannot know it,"[63] but none has considered the possibility that it is Yeats's acceptance of a fundamental truth in the Upaniṣads. In his *Memoirs* Yeats had recorded the same idea as coming from Mohini Chatterjee: the idea that truth was not something that could be conveyed from one man to another, because it was a state of mind.[64] There is a final stage of meditation in the Upaniṣads where there is no division between the knower and the known. To know the Self is to become it.

Lunar symbolism pervades Yeats's later poetry to such an extent that it sheds light even on poems where it is not mentioned explicitly. Many critics have offered insightful studies of the two Byzantium poems, of 'Among School Children,' 'A Dialogue of Self and Soul,' without going into their Upanisadic background. G.S. Fraser in his essay on 'Byzantium' in *Yeats: Poems, 1919–1935*, offers us the useful insight that Byzantium presents "a timeless and persistent order of some sort."[65] He, however, says that the Byzantium of the poem has not much to do with the historic Byzantium, in spite of Yeats's passages of description in *A Vision* that regard Byzantium as occurring at the full moon or the fifteenth phase, a phase of fulfilment.[66] We learn more about this phase when we read in Yeats's essay on 'The Holy Mountain': "I find my imagination setting in one line *Turīya*—full moon, mirror-like bright water, Mount Meru…"[67] Yeats discovered that the Upaniṣads present *Suṣupti* and *Turīya*, the highest states of consciousness achievable by man. These he interpreted in terms of the symbolism of the dark moon and the full moon respectively. An understanding of these states enables us to appreciate more comprehensively, 'A Dialogue of Self and Soul' as well as the Byzantium poems. *Suṣupti*, literally dreamless sleep, is the state wherein bliss is achieved though a total annihilation of personality, and surrender to a transcendent power. Yeats's Soul seeks as ideal a state wherein "all thought is done" and asks rhetorically, "Who can distinguish darkness from the soul?" The dark moon is a symbol of passivity in *A Vision*. On the other hand, the state of illumination wherein ultimate reality is apprehended is spoken of as *Turīya*. Yeats marked the following sentence in his copy of Radhakrishnan's *Indian Philosophy*: "Reality is different from thought, and can be reached in the *turīya* state of highest immediacy, which transcends thought and its distinctions, where the individual coincides with the central reality."[68] Ruth Nevo in 'Yeats's Passage to India' mistakenly writes that *Turīya* is the second stage in meditation.[69] *Turīya* (literally, "the fourth") is the final stage in meditation: it is a complete consciousness of unity represented by the symbol *aum* where there is identification between subject and object. According to the *Māṇḍūkya Upaniṣad* (verse 12):

> The fourth is that which has no elements, which cannot be spoken of, into which the world is resolved, benign, non-dual. Thus the syllable *aum* is the very self.

A simplistic comparison of *Turīya* and the full moon symbol leads Nevo and Hegde to see *Turīya* as the second stage, and the latter even wonders why a being should proceed to the dark moon after attaining enlightenment.[70] Yeats's symbol of the full moon came to stand for the state of enlightenment and unity wherein some expiation still needs to be undergone in future incarnations, as well as for the final state wherein "all old Karma exhausted," the yogi or the initiate achieves entire unity of being. This was discussed thoroughly by him in 'The Holy Mountain' and 'The Mandukya Upanishad' in *Essays and Introductions*.

The Upaniṣads advocate not rejection but control over all the faculties; the senses and the mind are to be used as instruments of the spirit. Yeats spoke approvingly of this "alliance between body and soul our theology rejects," because it echoed his own basic convictions.[71] In fact, our understanding of *Turīya* throws light on all poems and passages wherein Yeats speaks of a self-realised existence. The dancer in 'Among School Children' exemplifies the final fusion of body, mind, and spirit, whereas in thought or adoration, however exalted (Pythagoras, Plato, Aristotle, the nuns), a residue of the knower and the known remains. The full moon in *A Vision* is a phase of "the greatest possible beauty, being indeed that body which the soul will permanently inhabit, when all its phases have been repeated according to the number allotted...."[72] It is clear, then, that *Turīya* corresponds to Yeats's definition of Unity of Being as "a reality which is concrete, sensuous, bodily."[73] G.S. Fraser's aforementioned observation that Byzantium is about some kind of order stands endorsed and explained; the Byzantium poems can be seen to embody *Turīya*, this state of unified consciousness, as suggested in the chapter on "Unity of Being" in this book. Yeats saw that the dark moon and the full, *Suṣupti* and *Turīya*, are not only states of individual consciousness but may also be seen as objective and subjective phases in the history of civilizations.[74] Thomas R. Whitaker in *Swan and Shadow* states that "the psychological and religious situation is mirrored in history," and that Blake used the symbolism.[75] Yeats also saw that the Upaniṣads define the precise nature of the two states of consciousness that he could apply to civilizations.

Who were the beings that Yeats referred to as his "instructors" who gave to him the system of *A Vision*? Were they merely dramatizations of his own ideas and thoughts, external characterizations of internal voices? The next chapter, "Imagination," What the Upaniṣads Have Named "Self," deals with this intriguing matter. For many years Yeats attempted to achieve the trance state for his specific purposes as a poet. The theosophists presented the doctrine of the self as knowledge and power through practical occultism. One of its aspects was to train the would-be initiate to reach a state of omniscience. Yeats erroneously confused this with spirit-communication at séances, which, as noted earlier, the Theosophical Society disallowed. He carried on his quest as a member of the Golden Dawn evoking the Supreme Life through symbols. Harper in *Yeats's Golden Dawn* has made available the records of these proceedings in the Appendices to his book. So far no study has considered the connection between these records and Yeats's essay on 'Magic' in which he made public some of his conclusions about the powers of the mind as evidenced in telepathy and thought transference. His experiments in spiritism led him to ask whether the voices that were heard were internal or external to the mind. Another question related to images and symbols that appeared in the mind: which part of the mind did they arise from? The Society for Psychical Research upheld the rational view that telepathy among those present could alone explain these voices. Yeats rejected this with his "Preliminary Examination of the Script of ER" (published by Harper in *Yeats and The Occult)*, positing the definite conclusion that the communicating spirits were real and maintained their identity after death.[76] But this could in turn imply that there was no such thing as the mystical state in which messages came from the deeper self. Yeats was perplexed in spite of the fact that spirits could not convey profound truths; there was, he was sure, such a thing as revelation. Ellmann considers that Yeats's own encounter with spirits that gave him the system of *A Vision* may be understood in terms of Jung's concept of the racial unconscious or Henry More's *anima mundi*.[77] Yeats himself found the answers in the Upaniṣads. He learnt that there was a transcendental portion of the mind that was called *Ātman* or Self by the Upaniṣads; imagination was its faculty. It created the images that composed *anima mundi*, the images seen by mystics in their trance state. This enabled him to divide the communicating spirits into two categories: the spirits of the dead, and the liberated spirits with whom communication was possible by meditation. "A wise man seeks in Self," quoted Yeats from the *Chāndogya Upaniṣad*, "those that are alive and those that are dead and gets what the world cannot give."[78] In *A Vision* (1937), he substituted for *anima mundi*, the more comprehensive term *Celestial Body*. This was the state in which all forms copied by the poets were present as ideas. He concluded that psychical research was close to a main thought of the Upaniṣads. "Continental investigators, who reject the spiritism of Lodge and Crookes, but accept their phenomena, postulate an individual self possessed of such power and knowledge that they seem at every moment about to identify it with that Self without limitation and sorrow, containing and contained by all, and to seek there not only the living but the dead."[79] The power and knowledge of the self was imagination.

The final chapter has for its theme, "Yeats's View of Symbolism in the Light of the Upaniṣads." As Yeats moved away from a decadent poetic practice, he felt the need to hunt for forms and methods by which visionary truth must be conveyed. He realized that although it was difficult to translate experience into language, there was a possibility that it could be evoked through symbols. He found in the Upaniṣads a complete exposition of the philosophical and psychological principles of symbolism. Kathleen Raine has made the relevant point that in Yeats's work, "the scenery—the images—are those of his native Ireland,"[80] while the spiritual knowledge is that of India. This is true in fact, and I have explained in this chapter why "native scenery" was important to Yeats. The seers of the Upaniṣads regarded creation as a symbolic manifestation of the Creator; by meditating upon an object that is visible and familiar, one moves by degrees to the transcendental reality beyond it. So they devised the method of meditation upon symbol, a method in which waking, dream, and dreamless sleep become stages in meditation, finally leading to merger with the Absolute. *Hiraṇyagarbha* is the dream state of the macrocosm in which the mind of the Creator becomes filled with ideas and subtle forms of creation that are in turn reflected in the microcosm or individual in the dream state. So there is really one mind and one memory shared by all individuals at a certain level, and it is this common feature that makes communication possible. In his essay on 'Magic' Yeats speaks of this one mind and memory, which can be evoked through symbols.

Yeats realized that nature symbols like sun, moon, sea, etc. were universal, common to Eastern and Western traditions alike. He discovered that symbols given by his instructors in *A Vision* were of this kind. He knew that the symbol itself belonged to the concrete world of the waking state; the reader must move from this level to the next, that of understanding the meaning, the concept portrayed by the symbol. The meaning must then be pondered over and meditated upon. This process, if carried on with concentration, would itself reveal the experience that lay beyond. The reader would then share the poet's experience.

This study endeavours to substantiate and elaborate upon these key areas of Yeats's interest. Yeats found that as philosophy the Upaniṣads were of central importance. He wrote:

> Whatever the date, these forest Sages began everything; no fundamental problem of philosophy, nothing that has disturbed the schools to controversy, escaped their notice.[82]

In the present work, there is primarily an attempt to follow the thread of Yeats's thought as it gets increasingly entwined with the thought of the Upaniṣads. Yeats's interest in the Upaniṣads was part of his fundamental desire to turn literature away from a position where it only mirrored reality. "The end of art," he said, "is the ecstasy awakened by the presence before an ever-changing mind of what is permanent in the world...."[82] He found that the Upaniṣads were unique in offering wisdom that may have been available to the West long ago but had faded away during the course of the centuries.

> We have borrowed directly from the East and selected for admiration or repetition everything in our own past that is least European, as though groping backwards towards our common mother.[83]

Notes

1 George Mills Harper, *W.B. Yeats and W.T. Horton: The Record of an Occult Friendship* (New Jersey: Humanities Press, 1980), p.123. Hence cited as *Yeats and Horton*.

2 Elizabeth Cullingford, *Yeats: Poems 1919-1935* (London and Basingstoke: Macmillan Publishers Ltd., 1984), see pp. 59, 63, 49. Hence cited as Cullingford.

3 Graham Hough, *The Mystery Religion of W.B. Yeats* (Sussex: The Harvester Press Ltd., 1984), p.20. Hence cited as Hough.

4 See Cullingford, pp.9, 16, 21.

5 W.B. Yeats, *Autobiographies* (London: Macmillan and Co. Ltd., 1956), pp.265, 264.

6 Rabindranath Tagore, *Gitanjali* (London: Macmillan, 1912); Purohit Swāmi, *An Indian Monk, His Life and Adventures* (London: Macmillan, 1932), Purohit Swāmi, trans. from Marathi, Bhagwān Shri Hamsa's *The Holy Mountain* (London: Faber and Faber, 1934); Purohit Swāmi, trans. from Sanskrit, *Bhagwān Shri Patanjali: Aphorisms of Yoga* (London: Faber and Faber, 1938). The last three works are hence cited as *Indian Monk*, *Holy Mountain*, and *Patanjali*, respectively.

7 The word *upaniṣad* has been spelt in two ways throughout this book. While quoting some author the original spelling (i.e. upanishad) has been retained; otherwise, the international scheme of transliteration as indicated in S. Radhakrishnan's *The Principal Upaniṣads* (London: George Allen and Unwin, 1953), has been adhered to.

8 W.B. Yeats and Shri Purohit Swāmi, trans. from Sanskrit, *The Ten Principal Upanishads* (London: Faber and Faber, 1937). Hence cited as Yeats and Swāmi.

9 Richard Ellmann, *Yeats: The Man and the Masks* (1948; rpt. Middlesex: Penguin Books Ltd., 1987), p.71. Hence cited as *Man and Masks*.

10 H.R. Bachchan, *W.B. Yeats and Occultism* (Delhi: Motilal

Banarsidass, 1965). Hence cited as *Yeats and Occultism.*

11 Narayan Hegde, "W.B. Yeats and Purohit Swami: A Study of Yeats's Last Indian Phase," Ph.D. dissertation, State University of New York at Stony Brook, 1980. Hence cited as Hegde.

12 See Cullingford, p.16.

13 Hough, pp.35, 38.

14 Kathleen Raine, *Yeats the Initiate* (London: George Allen and Unwin Ltd., 1986), p.1. Hence cited as Raine.

15 *Ibid.*, p.331.

16 *Ibid.*,p.3.

17 See George Mills Harper, *Yeats's Golden Dawn* (London and Basingstoke: The Macmillan Press ltd., 1974), p.7; hence cited as *Golden Dawn.* Also see Raine, p.335.

18 W.B. Yeats, *Memoirs* (London and Basingstoke: Macmillan London Ltd., 1972), pp.23–24.

19 William Wynn Westcott's 'Historic Lecture to Neophytes of the Golden Dawn,' quoted in *Golden Dawn*, p.11.

20 *Memoirs*, p.24.

21 *Ibid.*, p.27. Westcott had also drawn a distinction between the abstraction of "the Eastern School of Theosophy and Occultism" and the "concretion of our own Hermetic Society of the G.D." See *Golden Dawn*, p.162, note 57.

22 See *Golden Dawn*, Appendix K.

23 *Memoirs*, p.282.

24 Harold Bloom, *Yeats* (New York: Oxford University Press, 1970), p.372. Hence cited as Bloom.

25 Thomas Parkinson, *The Later Poetry* (Berkeley: University of California Press, 1971), p.1. Hence cited as Parkinson.

26 *Autobiographies*, p.263.

27 W.B. Yeats, *Essays and Introductions* (London: Macmillan and

Co. Ltd., 1961) p.429. Hence cited as *Essays.*

28 *Autobiographies*, p.92.

29 Yeats and Swāmi, p.10.

30 *Memoirs*, p.42.

31 *Autobiographies*, p.490.

32 See Shalini Sikka, "W.B. Yeats and the Upaniṣads: An Introductory Note," in *Yeats Eliot Review*, XII.2 (1993), pp.56–60. This paper considers how the Upaniṣads came to be among Yeats's sources for ancient wisdom, and discusses briefly their relevance to Yeats's poetry.

33 Mohini Chatterjee, *Transactions of the London Lodge of the Theosophical Society* (London: Printed by C.F. Roworth, 1885), No.3, p.3. Hence cited as *Transactions.*

34 See Pierce Leslie Pielou, "The Growth of the Theosophical Society in Ireland," unpublished typescript no.38619 in The Theosophical Library, Adyar, Madras.

35 See Yeats and Swāmi, p.7.

36 *Essays*, p.293.

37 See *Autobiographies*, p.188.

38 See W.B. Yeats, *Mythologies* (London: Macmillan and Co. Ltd., 1972), p.343.

39 Ursula Bridge, ed., *W.B. Yeats and Sturge Moore: Their Correspondence* (London: Routledge and Kegan Paul Ltd., 1953), p.69. Hence cited as *Yeats and Sturge Moore.*

40 See W.B. Yeats, *A Vision* (London and Basingstoke: the Macmillan Press Ltd, 1937), p.12. Hence cited as *Vision* (B).

41 (a) W.B. Yeats, *A Vision* (T. Werner Laurie Ltd., 1925). Hence cited as *Vision* (A).

(b) See *Essays*, p.518: "Subconscious preoccupation with this theme brought me *A Vision.*"

42 R.E. Hume, *The Thirteen Principal Upanishads* (Oxford, 1921).

I have consulted the copy in Yeats's personal library, courtesy Ms. Anne Yeats. Hence cited as Hume.

43 Allen Wade, ed., *The Letters of W.B. Yeats* (London: Rupert Hart Davis, 1954), p.794. Hence cited as *Letters*.

44 Letter to Yeats written on 4 November 1935; Purohit Swāmi Papers, Nehru Museum and Library, New Delhi. Hence cited as Swāmi Ms.

45 *Letters*, p.806.

46 *Ibid.*, p.846.

47 *Ibid.*, p.839.

48 (a) Yeats's letter excerpted in Mokashi Punekar, *The Later Phase* in the *Development of W.B. Yeats* (Dharwar: Karnatak University, 1966), p.265. Hence cited as *The Later Phase*.

(b) Yeats had written a few months earlier to Shree Hamsa, who was Purohit Swāmi's master: "In a few days I shall send you the Translation of *The Upanishads* made by Shree Purohit Swāmi with my help. Later in the year a curious book of spiritual philosophy by myself." Unpublished letter written on 12 March 1937.

49 *Man and Masks*, p.230.

50 *Vision* (B), p.246.

51 Hough, p.13.

52 *Vision* (B), p.40.

53 See *Vision* (A), p.176.

54 *Ibid.*

55 *Man and Masks*, p.288.

56 *Īṣa Upaniṣad*, p. 1. All quotations from the Upaniṣads, unless otherwise stated, are from *The Principal Upaniṣads*.

57 *Letters,* p.844.

58 See *Memoirs*, p.266.

59 See *Vision* (B), p.220.

60 Raine, p.317.

61 *Ibid.*, p.304.

62 Bloom, p.375.

63 Parkinson, *The Later Poetry*, p.3.

64 See *Memoirs*, p.145.

65 See Cullingford, pp.207–217.

66 See *Vision* (B), p.279.

67 *Essays*, p.472.

68 S. Radhakrishnan, *Indian Philosophy* (London: George Allen and Unwin Ltd., 1923), I, 161. I have consulted the copy in Yeats's personal library, courtesy Ms. Anne Yeats.

69 See *Yeats Annual No.4* (Macmillan Literary Annuals), p.24.

70 See Hegde, p.119.

71 See *Essays*, p.451.

72 *Vision* (B), p.136.

73 *Ibid.*, p.214.

74 See *Essays*, p.471.

75 Thomas R. Whitaker, *Swan and Shadow: Yeats's Dialogue with History* (Chapel Hill: The University of North Carolina Press, 1964), p.22. Hence cited as *Swan and Shadow*.

76 See George Mills Harper, ed., *Yeats and the Occult* (London and Basingstoke: The Macmillan Press Ltd., 1976), pp.141–171.

77 Richard Ellmann, *The Identity of Yeats* (London: Oxford University Press, 1954), p.151. Hence cited as *Identity*.

78 *Essays*, p.509.

79 Yeats and Swāmi, p.9.

80 Raine, p.336.

[81] Yeats and Swāmi, p.11.

[82] *Essays*, p.287.

[83] *Ibid.*, p.433.

Chapter One

The Ten Principal Upanishads: Some Aspects of the Translation by Yeats and Purohit Swāmi

W.B. Yeats's desire to undertake the translation of the Upaniṣads was of personal as well as wider significance. Foremost, Yeats felt that the thought of the Upaniṣads had a direct bearing upon the themes of contemporary poetry, which was beginning to be less preoccupied with social criticism and like themes, and had begun to ask the most profound questions.[1] The Upaniṣads offered not only an understanding of problems arising out of psychical research, but dealt also with the fundamental problems of philosophy.[2] He explained to Dorothy Wellesley that all great poets sought a comprehensive system of thought in their different ways; the Upaniṣads offered such a philosophy:

> we need, like Milton, Shakespeare, Shelley, vast sentiments, generalizations supported by tradition. (Hence your allusions to Heraclitus and his contemporaries, my toil at the *Upanishads*...)[3]

It is obvious that Yeats's decision to assist the Swāmi in his translation of the principal Upaniṣads was prompted not only by his desire to absorb their thought fully, but also by his wish to make available their essence to young writers searching for similar ideas.

He was not much impressed by English translations of the original Sanskrit texts. None of the editions recommended by his friend George Russell was particularly attractive to him. For instance, Max Mueller's translations of the Upaniṣads in the series, *Sacred Books of the East* had appeared in 1884. Max Mueller's intention in presenting these translations was strictly that of a historian and scholar of religion and philosophy. He wrote in his Preface to the series that his intention was to place before historians and philosophers unembellished and accurate versions of some of the sacred books of the East.[4] He did not seem to be too concerned with reproducing the poetic character of the originals, and prepared the reader to encounter certain oddities of style like strange combinations of nouns and adjectives, very long or very abrupt sentences. The reason was that he was willing to sacrifice idiom to truth.[5]

That Yeats disapproved of such a translation is evident from his Preface to *The Ten Principal Upanishads*. (In fact one of the "eminent scholars" who left him "incredulous" may well have been Max Mueller.) Yeats emphasized that the Upaniṣads presented not only philosophy, but poetry of a high order, for they were sung long before they were written down. "When belief comes we stand up, walk up and down, laugh or swing an arm."[6] In other words, spontaneity and naturalness of expression are the best proof of belief, and indicate fidelity to the original inspiration. Yeats undertook to help the Swāmi in translating the Upaniṣads so that the text would read as if "the original had been written in common English."

The Upaniṣads are written for the most part in a cryptic, aphoristic style, requiring a commentary. Sanskrit in these scriptures is used as a language of spiritual science and contains, like any other science, certain technical terms and other words which scarcely admit of translation. The Yeats-Swāmi translation is written, as Yeats maintains, in natural English; explanatory notes, considered necessary for most translations of scriptures, have been done away with.

One of the ways in which Yeats achieved this was by substituting Western symbols for Eastern ones. For instance, in the *Īśa Upaniṣad* (spelt 'Eesha Upanishad' by Yeats), occurs the following verse:

> *hiraṇmayena pātreṇa satyasyāpihitam mukham tat tvaṁ pūṣan apāvṛṇu satyadharmāya dṛṣṭaye.* (*Īśa*, 15)

Its translation by Radhakrishnan, Hume, and Yeats and Swāmi is as follows:

(a) The face of truth is covered with a golden disc. Unveil it, O Pūṣan, so that I who love the truth may see it. (Radhakrishnan)

(b) With a golden vessel
The Real's face is covered over. (Hume)

(c) They have put a golden stopper into
The neck of the bottle. Pull it, Lord! Let

Out reality. I am full of longing. (Yeats and Swāmi)

Narayan Hegde in his thesis, 'W.B. Yeats and Purohit Swāmi,' explaining that "the golden disc" in the original suggests the dazzling sun that blinds us to the reality behind it, objects that "it is surprising that Yeats would ignore sun imagery, which was so close to his own fancy, in favour of 'a golden stopper into the neck of the bottle' that is so anachronistic to Upanisadic times."[7] There is evidence that at one stage Yeats wished to do away altogether with symbols. Yeats's own copy of *The Ten Principal Upanishads* has the following corrections of this verse:

They have put a golden stopper into
truth the neck of the ~~bottle~~. Pull it, Lord!
truth Let out ~~reality~~. I am full of longing.[8]

On 6 September 1937, he wrote to Purohit Swāmi about having made a correction "on p.17 line 1." "Instead of 'Let out reality' I have put 'Let out the truth.' This is to avoid the unmeaning use of truth and reality for the same thing in the same sentence."[9] However, the published version has none of these corrections. Yeats must have decided against the change after all. He probably felt that the use of the symbol (of the bottle) was justified as the idea of the verse would be easily grasped by the Western reader. In the Upaniṣads the sun is often used as a symbol of supreme intelligence, *Ātman* or *Brahman;* used thus it creates no confusion in the mind of the reader. In the present context, however, the phrase *hiraṇmayena pātreṇa* means really a golden disc or cover, an example of which may be the sun. Therefore, a translation that renders the golden disc or cover as the sun, conveys the idea that the sun veils the face of the truth, and confuses the reader by using the symbol in an unusual and non-prevalent sense. Yeats was aware that the "golden disc" would require to be glossed, as it is a symbol not merely of the sun but also of all that is attractive and tempting in the external world. Realizing that the essential idea must be conveyed, whatever the symbol, Yeats chose the symbol of "a golden stopper in the neck of the bottle," expressing the idea that the stopper, though golden and attractive, must nevertheless be removed before reality is tasted.[10] By means of this symbol, familiar to Western and Eastern readers alike, Yeats achieves entire intelligibility.

Also, Yeats avoids references to mythical figures, esoteric sacrificial ceremonies, and substitutes self-explanatory words instead. The last few verses of the *Īśa Upaniṣad* are a prayer for the vision of God and are chanted during funeral rites:

agne naya supathā rāye asmān . . . (*Īśa*, 18)

Radhakrishnan's translation reads:

O Agni, lead us, along the auspicious path to prosperity.

Yeats, in keeping with his purpose of rendering the spirit rather than the literal meaning of the verses translates the invocation to the funeral fire as "Holy Light."[11] Similarly in the *Kaṭha Upaniṣad* occurs the following line:

uśan ha vai vājaśravasaḥ sarva - vedasaṁ dadau (*Kaṭha*, I, 1.1)

Desirous (of the fruit of the Viśvajit sacrifice) Vājaśravasa, they say, gave away all that he possessed. (Radhakrishnan)

Wājashrawas, wanting heaven, gave away all his property.[12]
(Yeats and Swāmi)

Yeats substitutes the simple phrase "wanting heaven" for the specific ritual mentioned above, thus conveying the essential idea of the Upanisadic seer. In the same Upaniṣad occurs the following verse:

ṛtam pibantau sukṛtasya loke guhām praviṣṭau parame parārdhe,

chāyā-tapau brahma-vido vadanti, pañcāgnayo ye ca tri-ṇāciketāḥ.
(*Kaṭha*, I.3.1)

There are two selves that drink the fruit of Karma in the world of good deeds. Both are lodged in the secret place (of the heart), the chief seat of the Supreme. The knowers of *Brahman*, speak of them as shade and light as also (the householders) who maintain the five sacrificial fires and those too who perform the triple Nāciketas fire. (Radhakrishnan)

Yeats and Swāmi's rendering of the above is as follows:

The individual self and the universal Self, living in the heart, like shade and light, though beyond enjoyment, enjoy the result of action. All say this, all who know Spirit, whether householder or ascetic.[13]

Yeats translates "the knowers of Brahman" (*brahma-vido*) simply as "all who know Spirit." The word *Brahman* would need a gloss, so by using the word "Spirit," Yeats brings the translation in line with his own terminology in *Book II : The Completed Symbol* of *A Vision. Brahman* or *Spirit* is one of the four Principles in the Upaniṣads as well as in Yeats's system. In the same verse, references to the performers of the "triple Nāciketas fire" and the "five sacrificial fires," would not be readily understood by Western readers, as these terms were used by those adept in the lore of sacrifice and spirituality. In this context, Yeats's "householder or ascetic" adequately conveys the idea.

For *Indra*, a Hindu mythical figure and personification of lightning in the *Kena Upaniṣad* (III.11), Yeats and Swāmi substitute "Light."[14] In the *Chāndogya Upaniṣad, deva-asura* is translated by Hume as "the gods and the devils" and by Yeats simply as "the godly and the godless."[15] For *Svayambhūḥ* which means "self-caused," Yeats uses "God" (*Kaṭha Upaniṣad*, II. 1.1). For *Aditi*, a mythological figure representing mother nature or mother of Gods, Yeats substitutes "boundless Power," which is also the etymological meaning of *aditi* (as in the *Kaṭha Upaniṣad*, II.1.7). In the *Bṛhad-āraṇyaka Upaniṣad, gandharvalokā*, the world of aerial spirits, is rendered as "the region of the celestial choir."[16]

Some verses in the Yeats-Swāmi translation convey a clearer idea of the original than their counterparts in Radhakrishnan's or Hume's translations. For example, the *Bṛhad-āraṇyaka Upaniṣad* contains a fine definition of the self which begins:

> *sa vā ayam ātmā brahma, vijñānamayo manomayaḥ prāṇamayaś . . .*
> (*Bṛhad-āraṇyaka*, IV. 4.5)

Hume renders it thus :

> Verily, this soul is Brahma, made of knowledge, of mind, of breath...

Here the phrase "made of" is misleading, as the *ātman* is not "made of" anything external to it. Yeats and Swāmi render it in the following manner:

> This Self is Spirit. He is knowledge, mind, life... [17]

conveying the idea that these qualities are inherent in the Self. This rendering does not convey the meaning that the Self is a sum of its parts, an idea that might be derived from Hume's translation.

Another verse from the *Chāndogya Upaniṣad* may be examined:

> *ta ime satyāḥ kāmāḥ anṛtāpidhānāḥ, teṣāṁ satyānāṁ satām anṛtam*

apidhānam . . . (*Chāndogya,* VIII. 3.1)

These same are true desires, with a covering of what is false. (Radhakrishnan)

Yeats and Swāmi render it more clearly than Radhakrishnan in the following passage:

These wants are justified, but they are smothered by self-interest.[18]

To take another instance from the *Bṛhad-āraṇyaka Upaniṣad*:

tad yathā peśaskārī peśaso mātrām upādāya, anyan navataraṁ kalyāṇataraṁ rūpaṁ tanute, evam evāyam ātmā, idaṁ śarīraṁ nihatya, avidyāṁ gamayitvā, anyan navataraṁ kalyāṇataraṁ rūpaṁ kurute . . . .
(Bṛhad-āraṇyaka, IV. 4.4.)

And as a goldsmith, taking a piece of gold turns it into another, newer and more beautiful shape, even so does this self, after having thrown away this body and dispelled its ignorance, make unto himself another, newer and more beautiful shape... (Radhakrishnan)

And as a goldsmith takes the gold from an old piece of jewelry and shapes it into a more modern piece, so the Self forgets the old body, takes hold of another body...[19] (Yeats and Swāmi)

Here the phrase "Self forgets the old body" is closer to the original than Radhakrishnan's "having dispelled its ignorance." Consider also the following verse from the *Praśna Upaniṣad*:

tisro-mātrā mṛtyumatyaḥ prayuktā anyonya-saktā anavi-prayuktāḥ.
kriyasu bāhyābhyantara-madhyamāsu samyak-prayuktāsu nakampate jñaḥ.
(Praśna, V.6.)

The three elements (each) leading to death (by itself), if they are united to each other without being separated and employed in actions well performed, external, internal or intermediate, the knower does not waver. (Radhakrishnan)

Yeats and Swāmi in their translation render the idea with greater lucidity:

If man meditates on the three syllables in separation, it is the emblem of mortality; but if he meditate upon all together, inseparable, interdependent, the three conditions, physical, mental, intellectual, reward him; he goes beyond mortality.[20]

This version clearly indicates that a meditation upon the three syllables (of AUM, referred to in the preceding verse in the

Upaniṣad), combined into one word, not only rewards a man in the physical, mental and intellectual realms, but also bestows immortality upon him.

It will be observed, however, that occasionally due to over-simplification, some ideas do not get conveyed in all their complexity in the Yeats and Swāmi translation. For example, the *Kaṭha Upaniṣad* presents the symbol of creation as the inverted tree:

> *ūrdhva–mūlo'vak-śākha eṣo' śvatthas sanātanaḥ* (*Kaṭha,* II.3.1.)
>
> With the root above and the branches below (stands) this ancient fig tree.
> (Radhakrishnan)

In Yeats's translation we have "Eternal creation is a tree, with roots above, branches on the ground."[21] As creation itself is represented by the inverted branches of the tree, the word "ground" becomes redundant. Yet another example is the rendering of a verse from *Kaṭha Upaniṣad*:

> *yathodakam durge vṛṣṭam parvateṣu vidhāvati,*
> *evaṁ dharmān pṛthak paśyaṁs tān evānuvidhāvati.* (*Kaṭha*, II.1.14.)
>
> As water rained upon a height flows down in various ways among the hills; so he who views things as varied runs after them (distractedly).
> (Radhakrishnan)

Here is the Yeats and Swāmi version:

> As rain upon a mountain ridge runs down the slope, the man that has seen the shapes of Self runs after them everywhere.[22]

The original verse clearly implies that preoccupation with variety distracts the person from the Self, whereas in Yeats's translation the fact of running after variety is merely reported. Moreover, Yeats and Swāmi's rendering, though simplified, is likely to be misleading due to the inclusion of the phrase "shapes of Self"; this can lead the reader to wonder why a knower of Self and its shapes is regarded as ignorant. Here Radhakrishnan's literal translation does not confuse the reader, as it is natural that he who "views things as varied" should be distracted.

There are some other renderings which are not self explanatory and would not be entirely comprehensible to a reader. For instance, in the *Kaṭha Upaniṣad* is the following verse:

indriyebhyaḥ param mano manaṣas sattvam uttamam,
sattvād adhi mahān ātmā, mahato' vyaktam uttamam. (II. 3.7)

Beyond the senses is the mind; above the mind is its essence (intelligence); beyond the intelligence is the great self; beyond the great (self) is the unmanifest. (Radhakrishnan)

Yeats and Swāmi render it thus:

Mind is above sense, intellect above mind, nature above intellect, the unmanifest above nature.[23]

The idea in the verse is that which is "above" is really "finer than" or "subtler than" that which is below. The idea in the Upaniṣads is that the subtle pervades the gross (an idea discussed in the chapter on Nature). The philosophic aspect of the meaning is not fully conveyed in Yeats's translation; only a general idea of the hierarchy of the faculties is conveyed.

To take another example, in the *Kaṭha Upaniṣad* Naciketas asks: "Does He reflect another's light or shine of Himself?" And Yama the lord of death replies:

na tatra suryo bhāti, na candra-tārakam, nemā vidyuto bhānti, kuto'yam agniḥ:

tam eva bhāntam anubhāti sarvaṁ tasya bhāsā sarvam idaṁ vibhāti.
(*Kaṭha*, II,2.15.)

The sun shines not there, nor the moon and the stars, these lightnings shine not, where then could this fire be? Everything shines only after that shining light. His shining illumines all this world.[24] (Radhakrishnan)

Yeats and Swāmi render the passage thus:

Death replied: 'Neither sun, moon, stars, fire nor lightning lights Him. When He shines, everything begins to shine. Everything in the world reflects His light.'[25]

The idea, not so much stated as implied in the *Upaniṣad* is that the things that reflect His light cannot show Him. The senses work because of Him, they cannot reveal Him, an idea that became the theme of Yeats's poem 'The Statues.'[26] The lines: "What intellect,/ What calculation, number, measurement, replied?" convey the idea exactly. This theme is discussed exhaustively in the chapter on "Unity of Being." Yeats and Swāmi's translation reads like a eulogy of the Creator, without conveying the underlying philosophical idea.

In the *Muṇḍaka Upaniṣad*, Yeats and Swāmi have: "The Everlasting is…mindless"[27] In Hume too the same expression is used (*Muṇḍaka*, II.1.2). This word, unaccompanied by explanation, does not convey the actual meaning which is that the Absolute is not qualifiable in any way, and yet has potential for everything. Anothcr important idea in the Upaniṣads is that a man is considered wise when he ceases to identify himself with the body. Yeats and Swāmi express it thus: "A wise man, leaving his body, joins that flame; is one with His own nature."[28] Radhakrishnan explains that the phrase "rising out of the body" (used in his own translation) indicates ceasing to identify one's self with the body.[29] The phrase "leaving his body" in the Yeats-Swami translation does not convey the exact meaning.

There are certain junctures in the Upaniṣads where abstruseness of thought and brevity of expression occur together and call for a commentary. Yeats, however, wished to produce a translation that read well and could be independent of such commentary. It is a mark of his concern in this regard that he made the following corrections in his copy of the work before it was finally published.[30]

	Yeats's corrections in the margin	Verse	Margin
(a)		Because of his union with the Self and	
	unbroken	his ~~undecided~~ knowledge of it.	
		(*Māṇḍūkya*, 5)	
(b)	or	If he wants perfume ~~and~~ flowers	
	it	~~they~~ will appear	
	it	~~they~~ will appear (*Chāndogya*, VIII.2.6)	
(c)	we	~~I~~ swear by ~~my~~ soul	our
	we	~~I~~ must find that Self, by which	
	we	~~I~~ shall get whatever ~~I~~	we
	we	want, go wherever ~~I~~ like.	
		(*Chāndogya*, VIII.7.2)	

As we have observed earlier, Yeats's chief objective as a translator was that the text should read as though it had originally been composed in English. This idea stemmed from his basic conviction that no poet or writer could express himself well in a foreign language. As early as 1912 he was critical of Tagore's "monotony of sentence caused by (his) writing in a tongue not his native tongue."[31] His views on this subject had not changed in 1931 when he wrote to Rothenstein about Tagore:

> The only criticism I have to make upon him is that through the entire lack of judgment which I have noticed in others who belong to the Folk Life he published intolerable and interminable volumes of mistranslated verse instead of stopping after those first three fine books Sturge Moore and I corrected.[32]

It was with this idea in his mind that he advised Purohit Swāmi, when the latter had returned to India, to avoid Tagore's mistake. He warned the swāmi: "Do not attempt other books in English (the mistake that Tagore made with his poems) without some master of English or English scholar as your co-labourer."[33] In the case of the Upaniṣads, Yeats was translating from a foreign tongue into his own, and not into a foreign tongue as Tagore had done. The same idea was reinforced by Laura Riding who wrote to him, "I hope your *Upanishads* translate nicely into English sense."[34] In order to achieve this objective, Yeats strove to produce a translation that was independent of commentary and free of unintelligible jargon that he found in other translations. On this score Yeats was satisfied with the result:

> I have escaped that polyglot, hyphenated, latinised, muddied muddle of distortion that froze belief.[35]

His technique in translation is thus the reverse of his technique in poetry: whereas in his poetry he embellishes abstruse thought with racial symbols, in his translation he prunes away foreign metaphors and myths, and endeavours to endow the essential thought with a certain spontaneity of utterance. The intention in each case, however, is to express the unfamiliar in familiar terms. As noted earlier, he trained Purohit Swāmi too in this technique, explaining that a goddess was better referred to as "a pretty girl," instead of a "maiden of surprising loveliness." His fundamental advice was: "think like a wise man but express yourself like the common people...."[36] In the same letter he considered that theirs would be "the first great translation of the *Upanishads*." In a letter to Dorothy Wellesley he claimed that the Upaniṣads were translated as poetry for the first time.[37]

The Ten Principal Upanishads also provides evidence of the great interfusion between Yeats's own thought and that of the Upaniṣads.

Here are some examples:

> *Muṇḍaka Upaniṣad*, II.2.5:
>
> *yasmin dyauḥ pṛthivī cāntarikṣam otam manaḥ saha prāṇaiś ca sarvaiḥ...*
>
> He in whom the sky, the earth and the interspace are woven as also the mind along with all the vital breaths... (Radhakrishnan)
>
> Into His cloak are woven earth, mind, life, the canopy, the Kingdom of Heaven.[38] (Yeats and Swāmi)

Yeats uses "cloak" for "the sky, the earth..." a characteristic Yeatsian symbol for the not-self in *A Vision*[39] and in many plays.[40] This is an apt symbol as in the Upaniṣads too all creation is spoken of as the garb or "cloak" of the Creator, as the given quotation implies. Here is evidence that Yeats had completely mastered the similarities between his system and Upanisadic philosophy.

The *Muṇḍaka Upaniṣad* has the following verse:

> *hiraṇmaye pare kośe virajaṁ brahma niṣkalam*
> *tac chubhraṁ jyotiṣāṁ jyotiḥ tad yad ātma-vido viduḥ.* (II.2.10)

Hume's translation, which Yeats studied, rendered the same verse thus:

> In the highest golden sheath
> Is Brahma, without stain, without parts.

Yeats and Swāmi's translation is as follows:

> In a beautiful golden scabbard hides the stainless, indivisible, luminous Spirit.[41]

The word "scabbard" and the idea implied in "stainless" also form part of the imagery in Yeats's poem, 'A Dialogue of Self and Soul' where he says:

> The consecrated blade upon my knees
> Is Sato's ancient blade, still as it was,
> Still razor-keen, still like a looking-glass
> Unspotted by the centuries

Yeats refers to the Self as a razor-keen blade which shines like "a looking glass" and goes on to speak of the body as a "scabbard." By using the same words in his translation as well, Yeats provides an indication that the philosophy of the Upaniṣads underlies his own poem.

Again, in translating another verse from the same Upaniṣad (*Muṇḍaka*, III.2.7), Yeats takes recourse to his own terminology in *A Vision*:

> His phases return to their source, his senses to their gods, his personal self and all his actions to the impersonal imperishable Self.[42]
>
> (Yeats and Swāmi)

Yeats's translation makes it evident that he wished to indicate a clear correspondence between his symbolism of the phases of the moon as fragments of the self, and a similar idea in the Upaniṣads.

For his part Yeats was trying to translate the Upaniṣads chiefly as works of revelation, not only as works of philosophy. Max Mueller, while enumerating the qualifications required in a translator of the sacred books of the East had pointed out that it was important to achieve some degree of realization before the thoughts of the ancient seers could be translated properly: "We need not become Brahmans or Buddhists or Taosze altogether, but we must for a time, if we wish to understand, and still more, if we are bold enough to undertake to translate their doctrines."[43]

Yeats expressed the same sentiment in 'The Statues' when he said that "passion could bring character enough"; the theme of the poem is that only he who has himself undergone the "passion" of an intense experience can recognize its special features in the work of another. Yeats himself had reached the high state of receptivity in which "instructors" spoke to him and revealed the secrets of the universe: he had thus entered that area of experience wherein the seers of the Upaniṣads received revelations. Such a poet can understand and render the thought of the Upaniṣads with fidelity and spontaneity. In the Indian classical tradition this lofty position is occupied by Śaṁkara, who was not only a commentator of the Upaniṣads, but himself a sage and a seer. Yeats too shares these qualities, and is a sympathetic translator who manages to transmit the inspiration of the Vedic seers. The lacunae in the Yeats-Swāmi translation should not obscure its merits. To have reproduced the abstruse thought of the Upaniṣads in the language of the common man, as per Aristotle's advice is a remarkable achievement, made possible through the rare combination of Yeats's calibre and Purohit Swāmi's understanding.[44]

The prime importance of this work for a Yeats scholar is the light it throws on the philosophy of the Upaniṣads in *A Vision*, as well as on the later poems and plays of Yeats. Yeats wrote to Dorothy Wellesley that his intention to spend the winter with the Indian monk, Purohit Swāmi, working on the Upaniṣads was part of his plan to be "reborn in imagination." He wrote to Ethel Mannin in the same vein that he wished to make "a last song, sweet and exultant, a sort of European *geeta*, or rather my *geeta*, not doctrine but song."[45] As the work of translation proceeded he became aware that it enhanced his creativity: poems and plays written during this period are clear evidence of his fascination with the thought of the Upaniṣads and of the process of converting doctrine into song. Of *The Herne's Egg* he wrote to Dorothy Wellesley on December 16, 1935:

> Shri Purohit Swāmi is with me, and the play is his philosophy in a fable, or mine confirmed by him. Every afternoon I go through his translation of the *Upanishads*.[46]

The phrase "mine confirmed by him" indicates that Yeats had wholly accepted this philosophy and made it has own; he then proceeded to give it embodiment in the play. The play in turn inspired him to write lyrics; while composing the scenario of *The Herne's Egg* he wrote: "I am trusting to this play to give me a new mass of thought and feeling, overflowing into lyrics."[47] 'Supernatural Songs' are among the lyrics that were composed at this time. In 1936, soon after completing work on the translation, Yeats wrote 'Lapis Lazuli,' a poem about the philosophy of detached and joyful action upheld in the Upaniṣads. He wrote to Dorothy Wellesley that he considered this poem "almost the best I have made of recent years."[48] In the same letter he indicated that he was revising *A Vision* in proof, and planned to add a story about Michael Robartes, a character who confers the wisdom of the east on his friends. In the years following, he wrote 'The Statues' (April 9, 1938), *Purgatory* (1939), *The Death of Cuchulain* (1939), poems and plays inspired by thought of the Upaniṣads.

The examples given above are only clues to the connection between Yeats and the Upaniṣads. They are a sufficient indication, however, that an understanding of this philosophy would contribute to a closer understanding of Yeats.

Notes

1 See Yeats and Swāmi, p.9.

2 *Ibid.*, pp.9–11.

3 *Letters*, p.853. Letter written in April 1936. Yeats voiced the same sentiment in his Preface to the *Ten Principal Upaniṣads*; see p.10.

4 See Max Mueller, trans., *The Upanishads: The Sacred Books of the East* (Oxford: Clarendon Press, 1879, 1884), I, xix. Hence cited as Max Mueller.

5 *Ibid.*, p.xxviii.

6 Yeats and Swāmi, p.8.

7 Hegde, p.86.

8 Copy in possession of Anne Yeats, pp. 16, 17.

9 Unpublished letter.

10 Although such a rendering may elicit the response that the Upanisadic flavour of the original is lost, yet Yeats's preference indicates an important aspect of his view of the Upaniṣads. As noted earlier, Yeats wished that the translation read as though the originals had been written in common English.

11 Yeats and Swāmi, p.17.

12 *Ibid.*, p.25.

13 *Ibid.*, p.31.

14 *Ibid.*, p.22.

15 *Ibid.*, p.111.

16 *Bṛhad-āranyaka Upaniṣad*, III.6.1; Yeats and Swāmi, p.139.

17 Yeats and Swāmi, p.154.

18 *Ibid.*, p.109.

19 *Ibid.*, p.153.

20 *Ibid.*, p.46.

21 *Ibid.*, p.36.

22 *Ibid.*, p.34.

23 *Ibid.*, p.37.

24 Radhakrishnan's translation is followed by the commentary that the Supreme is the source of all light, and cannot be known by any earthly light or knowledge. *The Principal Upaniṣads*, p.641.

25 Yeats and Swāmi, p.36.

26 W.B. Yeats, *Collected Poems* (London: Macmillan and Co. Ltd., 1978), p.375.

27 Yeats and Swāmi, p.52.

28 *Ibid.*, p.109.

29 See *The Principal Upaniṣads*, p.496.

30 Yeats and Swāmi; Yeats's copy, (a) p.60, (b) p.108, (c) p.111.

31 Yeats Ms. No.5918, letter No.33, National Library of Ireland.

32 *Ibid.*, letter No.48.

33 Unpublished letter.

34 G.M. Harper, R. Finneran, and W. Murphy, Eds., *Letters to W.B. Yeats* (London and Basingstoke: The Macmillan Press Ltd., 1977), p.611. Hence cited as *Letters to Yeats*.

35 Yeats and Swāmi, p.8.

36 *Letters*, p.846.

37 *Ibid.*, p.853.

38 Yeats and Swāmi, p.53.

39 *Vision* (B), p.232: "The *Celestial Body* is the Divine cloak lent to all, it falls away at the consummation and Christ is revealed."

40 See W.B. Yeats, *At the Hawk's Well*, *Collected Plays* (London: Macmillan and Co. Ltd., 1934), pp.208, 216.

41 Yeats and Swāmi, p.54.

42 *Ibid.*, p.56.

43 Max Mueller, I, xxxvii.

44 That the Yeats-Swāmi translation is now regarded as a standard modern translation is evidenced by the fact that William Gerber selected it for inclusion in his anthology, *The Mind of India.* For details see Vinod Sena, Ed. *The Autobiography of An Indian Monk* (New Delhi: Munshiram Manoharlal Pvt. Ltd., 1992), p.xxiii, Sena's footnote.

45 *Letters*, p.836.

46 *Ibid.*, p.844.

47 *Ibid.*, p. 845. Letter to Ethel Mannin on December 19, 1935.

48 *Ibid.*, p.859. Letter written on July 26, 1936.

Chapter Two

Yeats's View of Nature in the Light of the Upaniṣads

It is interesting to note that although Yeats himself moved from the empirical to the mystical method of understanding nature, he made the conflict between the two modes as they affect human life the study of a lifetime. As a schoolboy he was taught to study nature through his power of observation. In *Autobiographies* he recorded his experience of collecting moths and butterflies and studying his favourite book which described strange sea-creatures the scientist had found among the rocks.[1] He planned to write a book about creatures in the rocks, and the changes seen in them over a year, and in line with his empirical studies and under the influence of his father, he read Darwin and Wallace, Huxley and Haeckel.

There was, however, a significant change in his attitude to nature study when he realized that he knew very little despite all his years of collecting, so his interest in science began to fade.[2] This change was brought about by his contact with psychical research and mystical philosophy, which enabled him to break away from his father's influence.[3] He now discovered that of the two modes, the empirical maintained a constant separation between subject and object, while the mystical was intuitive implying that reality could be apprehended through imagination which transcended the subject-object duality. Yeats realized that the latter mode was a higher and surer pathway to reality, and found in mystical studies confirmation of his secret thoughts, and in Mohini Chatterjee's Vedantic philosophy explanations that confirmed his vague speculations.[4]

This change in Yeats's views became obvious in his opposition to his father's ideal of the subject of art. J.B. Yeats's view that he must paint what he could see was, according to Yeats, a misunderstanding created by Victorian science. Yeats thought that beautiful things should be painted, and regarded as beautiful only ancient things and dreams. By ancient things Yeats meant sacred tradition which did not look to empirical proof for support; he began occasionally telling people that one should believe whatever had been universally believed in, instead of only believing what could be proved.[5] In 'The Autumn of the Body' he recorded that he initially wished to describe outward things vividly, but suddenly lost the desire to do so, as he realized that externality introduced by scientific and political thought into literature had to be discarded.[6]

The rejection of materialism and positivism, and affirmation of mysticism were also aspects of the thought of Madame Blavatsky. She repudiated the methods of perception upheld by Tyndall, Huxley, and Haeckel, the philosophers studied so avidly by Yeats in his early years. In *Lucifer* she pointed out that obtaining knowledge by experiment was a very tedious method for those who aspired to do some real work, and emphasised the higher evidence of intuition.[7] Another theosophist, A.P. Sinnett, also asserted that it was worthwhile exploring the records accumulated by those who had penetrated the unseen.[8] To them, as it was to become for Yeats, sacred tradition was of great value. Madame Blavatsky deplored the inadequacy of the scientists' methods and their failure to explain the origin of matter and life. In *The Secret Doctrine* she referred to Tyndall's confession about the powerlessness of science in understanding even the world of matter, and to his doubt whether the scientists themselves possessed the intellectual powers which would enable them to grasp the ultimate structural bases of nature.[9] Yeats referred in *Autobiographies* to Huxley and Tyndall whom he detested, and confessed being made angry by the followers of Huxley, Tyndall, Carolus Duran, and Bastien-Lepage.

Against this background it is interesting to note that the empirical mode is referred to in the Upaniṣads as the waking state, and opposed to it is the mystical mode, the state of trance or revelation. The *Bhagavad-Gītā* sums up the two modes succinctly:

> What is night for all beings is the time of waking for the disciplined soul; and what is the time of waking for all beings is night for the sage who sees (or the sage of vision).[10]

Madame Blavatsky echoed this thought in *Isis Unveiled* when she said that "the life of the interior spirit is the death of external nature; and the night of the physical world denotes the day of the spiritual."[11] The publisher's note in Charles Johnston's *From the Upanishads* also summed up the view of the Upaniṣads: "Many of the Upanishads... so far from inculcating the literal fulfilment of the law, uphold in opposition the larger doctrines of inward religion."[12] This note throws light on the theme of contrasting modes of perception worked out by Yeats in his early plays, *Where There is Nothing*, its later version *The Unicorn from the Stars,* and *The Hour Glass*. In *Where there is Nothing* Yeats presented the opposition between a life devoted to useful things, organization, law as external authority, "entire submission," and a life of idleness, wandering, and internal authority.[13] Father John in *The Unicorn from the Stars* also indicates the contrast between the two modes: "it is to those who are awake that nothing happens, and it is they that know nothing. He is gone where all have gone for supreme truth."[14] On the other hand, the Wise Man in *The Hour Glass* mocks at the view that the spiritual kingdom can be known only when the faculties wither away. For him sensory perception is the only method of apprehending reality.

Yeats came in touch with the theory of creation in the work of the theosophists but understood only certain aspects of it in the early stages of his career. In 1893, in his work on Blake, he showed his awareness of the microcosmic aspect of creation. He wrote of Blake's "Golgonooza" that it was "situated on the point where the translucent becomes the opaque...It is the microcosmic aspect of that 'circle Pass not' so much talked of in Theosophical mysticism and is identical with the egg of Bramah—images of all things are contained within it."[15] The circle "Pass-Not" had been explained by Madame Blavatsky in *The Secret Doctrine*. According to her, "This world is the symbol (objective) of the ONE divided into the many ...and this One is the collective aggregate, or totality, of the principal Creators or Architects of this visible universe."[16] Yeats understood it as a stage in meditation where the mystic sees the images of all things, not perhaps as an important aspect of the macrocosm in which ideas are present before they become manifest as the concrete world.

The Vedic idea about the origin of the Universe was present in theosophical works as well as in translations of the Upaniṣads. The intelligent primordial source of the objective universe had been explained for the first time in the history of philosophy in the *Ṛg Veda sūtras* or hymns. According to the *Brahmanaspati Hymn*, "Existence, in the earliest age of Gods from non-existence sprang." The same view of creation was also presented in the *Chāndogya Upaniṣad*:

> In the beginning this [world] was non-existent. It became existent.[17]

The Sanskrit word for non-existent is *asat* and does not mean absolute non-being. It is a state in which "name and form" were not manifested. Basing his theme on this idea, the writer of the article, "Occultism and Modern Science" in *The Irish Theosophist*, explained that according to the Vedantins the origin of the universe was a primordial element or conscious directing soul, and "this endowment with intelligence of what our modern scientists regard as unconscious force seems to be the greatest difference separating the most advanced theories of today from the teaching of the ancients."[18] This idea is illustrated in the Upaniṣads through the parable of the student asked by his teacher to split open extremely fine seeds and declare what he found within. When he replies that he sees nothing at all, the teacher explains, "that subtle essence which you do not perceive…from that very essence this great *nyagrodha* tree exists."[19] The idea illustrated therein was that the cosmic process with its multiformity of names and forms arose from the subtle essence of Pure Being. Yeats was familiar with this episode as it formed a part of Charles Johnston's *From the Upanishads.*

A glance at Yeats's subsequent work shows that he seized upon this mysterious "nothing" as being inextricably linked to God. In 1897 he published a short story entitled 'Where There is Nothing, There is God.' In the short story it is not the Christian Brothers but the old beggar, who is shown to have discovered this truth; he is referred to as "Aengus the Lover of God," who has "found the nothing that is God."[20] In *The Unicorn from the Stars* Yeats presented the contemporary opposition between the materialist view that where there was no matter there was nothing, and the mystical vision of "nothing" as the indefinable, inexplicable essence or origin of matter. Paul Rutledge chooses "a religion so wholly supernatural that is so opposed to the order of nature that the world can never capture it," and finally cries out, "Colman, remember, where there is nothing there is God."[21] In *The Unicorn from the Stars*, the hero who has replaced Paul, affirms the same idea in Act III. That Yeats understood this "nothing" or *asat* only partly at this stage is evident from the fact that he found it difficult to understand the system of thought revealed to him by his instructors. This very "nothing" emerged as the symbol of the "sphere" in the automatic script but it would take Yeats a long time and much familiarity with the thought of the Upaniṣads before he understood it entirely.

In the 1925 version of *A Vision* Yeats made a brief mention of the *Four Principles* in terms of the different aspects of individuality or the microcosm. Of the *Principles* as aspects of creation in the macrocosm, he remarked significantly:

> I have not considered the ultimate origin of things, nor have my documents thrown a direct light upon it....I am inclined to discover in the *Celestial Body*, the *Spirit*, the *Passionate Body*, and the *Husk*, emanations from or reflections from his [Plotinus's] One, his Intellectual Principle, his Soul of the World, and his Nature respectively. The *Passionate Body* is described as that which links one being to another, and that which rescues the *Celestial Body* from solitude, and this is part of the office of the Soul of the World in Plotinus.[22]

This is an important paragraph and calls for a few observations. First, although Yeats saw the parallels between his *Principles* and neo-Platonic philosophy, he was not sure whether to accept the evolutionist or idealist position of the instructors (the phrase "emanations from or reflections from his One" indicates this). He also noted that there was a fundamental difference, between the system and that of Plotinus: "In Plotinus the One was the Good, whereas in the system Good and Evil were eliminated" before the Soul could be united to reality. Second, Yeats did not indicate clearly the relation between the *Principles* and the *Faculties*. He was aware, therefore, that he had to seek the answer to those problems in some source other than Plotinus. Some of his letters to Sturge Moore also show his awareness of the problems. "What is the sphere? What are the gyres?"[23] he wrote in June 1928.

His study of the Upaniṣads carried on over several years, before meeting Purohit Swāmi as well as in the latter's company afterwards, helped him to see in the *Four Principles* the explanation of both the macrocosm and microcosm in a detailed manner. This understanding is evident not only in the revised version of *A Vision*, but also in *The Herne's Egg* and many later poems including 'Supernatural Songs.'

Yeats's *Four Principles* can be compared to the four stages of creation described in the *Ṛg Veda* and the Upaniṣads. According to the Vedic view the reality at the root of the multiformity of the universe is formless. The *Ṛg Veda* describes it as indiscrete, harmonious, abstract, unique in itself, always alive by itself and without any counterpart, below, above or parallel. Through inner fervour the unique harmonious abstract projected the concept of oneness on it. This is the stage of the First Being or Supreme Being (*Īśvara*). The Supreme Being, through his desire imagined a creation which then became manifest, and through this process the formless, abstract reality assumed form.[24] The third stage is that in which notional forms appear in the mind of the Creator, and in the fourth these images take on concrete reality. These four stages of creation are rendered mythological in the Upaniṣads; the *Bṛhad-āraṇyaka Upaniṣad*, for instance, speaks of there being only the self in the beginning. This self said "I am." Then he divided himself into two, "became as large as a woman and man in close embrace. From their union human beings were produced."[25] This mythological explanation of creation also posits four principles, referred to in the Upaniṣads as *Brahman* (Absolute), *Īśvara* (the Lord or Creator), *Hiraṇya-garbha* (the golden womb of the world), and *Virāt* (the world). Radhakrishnan (whose *Indian Philosophy* Yeats read) explained the four principles thus: "Brahman is the simple, individual, absolutely self-identical, One, without a second. Once He is looked at as the creator or Īśvara, again as the Created or *Hiraṇyagarbha*....The body of the Virāt is made of the material objects in their aggregate....Prior to the evolution of the Virāt must have occurred the evolution of the Sūtrātman, the cosmic intelligence or Hiraṇyagarbha, having for his vehicle the totality of subtle bodies....In the form of Virāt, Hiraṇyagarbha becomes visible."[26]

In the revised version of *A Vision*[27] Yeats moved closer to the Upaniṣads. His view that ultimate reality, being neither one nor many, "can be symbolized but cannot be known" corresponds to the view of *Brahman* as formless, abstract, indescribable.[28] It is non-dual, *advaita*. Yeats symbolizes it as a "phaseless sphere" because it pervades all; there is nothing outside it. The Creator is also referred to in the *Kaṭha Upaniṣad* and elsewhere as self-existent or *svayambhūh*, self-created or *sukṛtam*, corresponding exactly to Yeats's *Spirit*, or "that which depends only upon itself." Yeats's *Celestial Body* as "the Divine Ideas in their unity," corresponds to *Hiraṇyagarbha*. *Passionate Body*, says Yeats, "is the present, creation, light, the objects of sense;" it is the created universe. *Husk* and *Passionate Body* are the subjective and objective aspects of this universe as they are "sense and the objects of sense." The Upaniṣads present an idealistic view of creation: the world is a manifestation of the imagined ideas of the Creator. In *The Hour Glass* Yeats had presented a similar view. The Wise Man's speech,

> I cry
> That what so God had willed
> On the instant be fulfilled...[29]

is an echo of both the Biblical, "God said, Let there be light: and there was light," and the Upanisadic reference to God's creation of water.[30]

As we have seen above, the Vedas and the Upaniṣads emphasize the idealistic view of creation. There is a myth in the *Brahmanaspati Hymn* of the *Ṛg-Veda* wherein we have, "Dakśa was born of Aditi, and Aditi was Dakśa's child."[31] In this myth the idea of the Creator first creating a progeny and then uniting with it is presented. In Yeats's play *The Herne's Egg* too we have a similar, somewhat puzzling verse:

> I lay with the Great Herne, and he,
> Being all a spirit, but begot
> His image in the mirror of my spirit,
> Being all sufficient to himself
> Begot himself...32

This verse clearly indicates that Attracta is not only the bride but also the daughter of the Herne. In all three myths A is the father of B, yet B is the mother of A. The underlying idea is that B being produced by A can only reproduce A in a different form.[33] This idea indicates the integral unity of the Creator, his creative faculty, and the product created. Such myths were formulated by the Vedic seers to explain the otherwise incommunicable idea of the apparent difference, yet essential unity of cause and effect. An interesting illustration of Yeats's belief in the idealistic theory of creation is the poem 'Leda and the Swan.' Though apparently about a historical cycle beginning with the rape of Leda by Zeus, at a deeper level it is about a creation cycle. The myth of Leda and Zeus has a close parallel in the myth of Brahma and Shatrupa in the *Bṛhad-āraṇyaka Upaniṣad* wherein Brahma created Shatrupa, and united with her. Thus human beings were produced.[34] She changed form but Brahma doing likewise pursued her and thus various creatures were born. Brahma, a spiritual entity evolved out of *Brahman*; in other words, the imminent descended from the transcendent, and created Shatrupa out of his idea or imagination. God created nature and entered her. "He the *Ātman* entered in here even to the tips of nails, as a razor is hidden in the razor case."[35] The resistance of Leda in one instance, and the flight of Shatrupa in the other, illustrate the idea that nature seems to flee, or to be separate from Spirit which has created it and controls it. Yeats mastered this mode of expression of the Vedic and Upanisadic sages and proceeded to create further myths along the same lines in 'Supernatural Songs.' In 'Ribh Denounces Patrick' he wrote:

> Man, woman, child (a daughter or a son),
> That's how all natural or supernatural stories run.
> . . .
> But all that run in couples, on earth, in flood or air, share God that is but three,
> And could beget or bear themselves could they but love as He.[36]

In this poem, as in the Upaniṣads, "love" or "desire" of the Supreme is responsible for creation. "Man" corresponds to the Supreme Spirit, "woman" to his creative power that is an inherent part of Spirit, and "child" to the created world that is the product of the interaction between the Creator and his creative faculty, for "God...is but three." In the light of this philosophy it becomes possible to decipher the symbols in Yeats's poem, 'What Magic Drum?'

> He holds him from desire, all but stops his breathing lest
> Primordial Motherhood forsake his limbs, the child no longer rest,
> Drinking joy as it were milk upon his breast.[37]

In these lines there are clear echoes of some Ṛg Vedic hymns as well as the myths of the Upaniṣads. One of the Ṛg Vedic hymns describes that in the state before creation the One breathed "breathless" and there was nothing else.[38] This is the state in which desire and breathing are held in abeyance, and it is natural that they soon become operative.

Similarly, "primordial motherhood" or the inherent desire to create is also dormant in Him, as is the "child" or creation. Another hymn in the *Ṛg Veda* describes non-being (*asat*) as lying "with outstretched feet" like a woman in the throes of childbirth.[39] Like the seers of the Vedas and the Upaniṣads Yeats wishes to portray the concept of idealistic creation, of the unity that binds the Creator and his creation.

It is possible to interpret the relationship between the Herne and Attracta in *The Herne's Egg* in the light of the myths of creation, which explain the macrocosmic principles in the Upaniṣads. The Herne is Yeats's name for *Haṁsa*, the principle at the base of the universe. In the Upaniṣads, *haṁsa* means "swan" as well as "That I am." The *Bṛhad-āraṇyaka Upaniṣad* refers to the spirit of the universe as "the golden person, the lonely swan."[40] The *Haṁsavati Hymn* of the *Ṛg Veda* refers to the Supreme Spirit as the swan in the sky.[41] In *The Herne's Egg* Yeats directs that in the opening scene a rock, its base hidden in mist, "should be suggested, not painted realistically."[42]This clearly implies that the principle at the base of the universe is indescribable and can only be represented symbolically. The Herne is referred to as "all sufficient to himself,"[43]the phrase indicating that he is the "causeless cause." Attracta as the bride of the Herne is imagination or the creative faculty of the Herne and is, therefore, an inherent part of him; her phrase, "I lay with him," implies a stage in which the creative faculty is latent in the Creator but is capable of becoming active. The imagined objects serve as a body of mind during the period of imagination. Hence Yeats's phrase, *Celestial Body* in *A Vision*.[44] When the mind is withdrawn from imaginary objects, they cease to exist. Attracta says she is "all a womb and a funeral urn,"[45] meaning that her birth, existence, and death depend on the Herne who has created her through his imagination. Thus the *Celestial Body* of ideas is the Herne's egg. (Yeats also says that Love and War, Concord and Discord, came from the eggs of Leda.[46]) The principles of separation and unification are latent in the mind of the Creator. It creates and separates, or unifies and dissolves periodically. In other words, the faculty of imagination is active and dormant by turns. When it is dormant there is no creation and the created world vanishes. *Muṇḍaka Upaniṣad* has the following verse: "As a spider sends forth and draws in (its thread)...so from the Imperishable arises here the universe."[47] Purohit Swāmi referred to this as "The emergence of this world from Spirit. The merger of this world into Spirit again."[48] Like the *Ṛg Veda* and the Upaniṣads, Yeats also uses the symbol of the Universe as egg. Michael Robartes, one of Yeats's imaginary characters in *A Vision* says that the universe is "a great egg that turns inside-out perpetually without breaking its shell...."[49] Not only does the great egg turn inside out but also "outside in." The latter phrase is not used by Yeats but is certainly implied in his use of Blake's phrase, "the pulsation of an artery" in his introduction to *A Vision* (1937).

Another question that interested Yeats was one on which the Upanisadic seers also speculated: why is there creation at all? The myths in the Upaniṣads explain creation as an attempt of the Supreme Being to assuage His loneliness and fear; it is also the result of His desire for companionship:

> He was afraid. Therefore one who is alone is afraid....He, verily, had no delight. Therefore, he who is alone has no delight. He desired a second.[50]

This view is paralleled by the explanation given by Yeats's instructors. According to them *Passionate Body* or nature exists that it may "save the *Celestial Body* from solitude."[51] In *The Herne's Egg* Attracta says that "Whatever shape he choose,/ Though that be terrible,/ Will best express his love."[52] According to Kate, the Herne's egg is a "mystery to make love-loneliness more sweet."[53] "He holds him from desire," but for how long? When the magic drum begins to beat, the cosmic will asserts itself and there is creation, the "beast has licked its young." Magic is Yeats's word for imagination and is synonymous with *maya* or the power of creation.[54] Yeats conveys the idea that creation is the result of the magical power inherent in the Creator, and it is but natural that this power expresses itself. As noted earlier, Yeats also uses the words "desire" and "love" to explain creation in 'Supernatural Songs.'

The interpretation of the myth wherein *Ātman* created, as "he had no delight," is that ultimate reality has two attributes: mobility and immobility, rest and creation, also symbolized as the day and night of Brahma. Gaudapāda, a classical philosopher-critic (in his famous commentary on the *Māṇḍūkya Upaniṣad*[55]), interprets the myth to mean that it is the innate aspect (*svabhāva*) of the ultimate to create. This inherent nature is what we perceive as Nature. This urge for creation is also the theme of 'What Magic Drum.' Yeats also quotes Paul Valéry as saying that Creation is pure work, "ouvrages purs d'une éternelle cause."[56]

From "Nothing" issues One or *Hiraṇyagarbha*, seen by Yeats as the egg of Leda or Concord. From this One is created Nature, multiformity or Discord. Yeats says in *A Vision* that Concord fashions all things into a homogeneous sphere.[57] the *Bṛhad-āraṇyaka Upaniṣad* explains Concord as the one common link that runs through all the multiformity of the world: "This indemonstrable and constant being can be realized as one only."[58] Radhakrishnan explains it as homogeneous pure intelligence without any break in it like space. Discord, on the other hand separates the elements and creates the world we inhabit, continues Yeats; this process of evolution of the world from the elements created by the Absolute is clearly explained in the *Taittirīya Upaniṣad*:

> From this Self verily, ether arose; from ether air; from air fire; from fire water; from water the earth; from the earth herbs; from herbs food; from food the person.[59]

All things, says Yeats, "fall into a series of antinomies in human experience...."[60] The Upaniṣads explain this by saying that the macrocosm and the microcosm, though composed of identical principles, appear to the human mind as divided into subject and object. Yeats presents this conflict through the symbolism of the interlocking cones, subject and object, Concord and Discord. Radhakrishnan explains how the microcosm can be analysed into four states of the soul reflecting the macrocosmic principles:

Subject (*Ātman*)	Object (*Brahman*)
1. The bodily self (Viśva)	1. Cosmos (Virāt or Vaiśvānara)
2. The Vital self (Taijasa)	2. The soul of the world (Hiraṇyagarbha)
3. The intellectual self (Prājña)	3. Self-consciousness (Īśvara)
4. The intuitive self (Turīya)	4. Ānanda (Brahman).[61]

The following comment by Radhakrishnan is underlined by Yeats in his copy of *Indian Philosophy*:

> The three conditions of the self, waking, dreaming, sleeping, together with

> that which comprehends them all, are called respectively the Viśva, the Taijasa, the Prājña and the Turīya states.[62]

Bṛhad-āraṇyaka Upaniṣad explains that the principles appear as antinomies when the sense of identity between macrocosm and microcosm is lost; the self is identified with the understanding, mind, life, sight, hearing, earth, water, air, ether; it is light and absence of light, desire and absence of desire, and so on.[63] Yeats says that the human individual may be seen as composed of the *Four Principles: Husk, Passionate Body, Spirit,* and *Celestial Body.* He explains that *Husk and Passionate Body* are senses and their objects, and *Spirit* and *Celestial Body* are mind and its object, that is, ideas. The above mentioned reference to the self from the *Bṛhad-āraṇyaka Upaniṣad* indicates that both senses and their objects are composed of the elements, and mind is ultimately the ideas which it grasps. *Kaṭha Upaniṣad* also refers to the *Principles* in the same manner.[64]

Book II of *A Vision*, entitled 'The Completed Symbol,' is extremely cryptic; definitions of the *Principles* are a little blurred and tend to overlap.[65] A comparative study of the *Principles* and the concept of sheaths or *Kośas* in the Upaniṣads throws a great deal of light on Yeats's ideas. In the Upaniṣads it is held that the body, mind, intellect, and bliss are really sheaths in which the self is encased. This concept is expounded in detail in the *Taittirīya Upaniṣad*.[66]

Husk, as the physical body with its senses, corresponds to *annamaya kośa* or the sheath made of food. In a footnote Yeats refers to active and passive senses spoken of in Indian philosophy.[67] These in the Upaniṣads are organs of action (*karmendriyas*: walking, etc.) and organs of knowledge (*jnānendriyas*: seeing, hearing, etc.). These are the motor and the sense organs which make up the gross body. When Yeats goes on to say that *Husk* is (a) "symbolically the human body," (b) the past, and (c) race or instinct, he appears to be using *Husk* as an umbrella term covering meanings that do not seem to be directly related. However, the links among them become clearer when we refer to the Upaniṣads. The Upaniṣads explain that the human body itself is an effect of some of the past actions of the individual. As the *Bṛhad-āraṇyaka Upaniṣad* has it, the self after death takes another, newer and more beautiful form of the manes, demigods, or higher beings. The *Viṣṇu Smṛiti* gives us the same idea: "…the soul of man puts on new bodies which are in accordance with its acts in a former life."[68] *Husk* and *Passionate Body*, says Yeats, are senses and the objects of senses. The *Aitareya Upaniṣad* explains how man's organs are composed of the elements. Fire as speech enters the mouth, air as breath enters the nostrils, the quarters of space become hearing and enter the ears, the moon becomes the mind/heart, and water becoming the semen enters the generative organ.[69] Thus the senses and their objects are really subjective and objective aspects of the same principle.

Husk, according to Yeats, is the past, not merely because objects are passed before we can know their images, but because those "images fall in patterns and recurrences shaped by a past life or lives."[70] *Husk* is the past and derives its name from the husk that is cast off by the sprouting seed, explains Yeats. Annie Besant had explained this in *Reincarnation and Karma,* saying that just as an accountant, closing the year's ledger, and opening a new one, did not transfer all the items of the old but only its balances, so the spirit passes on to the new brain only judgements and conclusions on the experiences of a life that is closed.[71] Thus *Husk* is comparable to the Indian concept of *saṁskāra* which means both impression on the memory as well as its effect.[72] *Husk*, therefore, is not only that past whose visible or symbolic result is the body, but also that which determines the manner in which an individual records impressions of the present. As these past experiences include actions of the individual performed as member of a race, therefore Yeats maintains that *Husk* is identified with race or instinct.[73] Here again it corresponds to *saṁskāra* as racial tradition.

Passionate Body is (a) the objects of sense, (b) the "sum of those *Daimons*" that an individual is trying to reach out to, (c) identical with physical light, and (d) exists, as discussed earlier, that it may "save the *Celestial Body* from solitude." Yeats sums it up as "the present, creation, light, the objects of sense."[74] *Passionate Body* is thus clearly analysable into its subjective and objective aspects. In its subjective aspect, *Passionate Body* corresponds firstly to the sheath of vital breath or *prāṇamaya kośa*; this is because Yeats sees it as "sensation," and the sheath of vital breath keeps the senses working and conveys their impressions to the mind. Secondly, it overlaps with the next sheath in the Upaniṣads, the sheath of the mind. The mind in the Vedas and the Upaniṣads is *antaḥkaraṇa*, literally inner organ or *manomaya kośa*. *Antaḥkaraṇa* too is comprehensive, as according to the *Yajurveda* it combines four functions: *manas* or perception and sensation; *ahaṁkāra*, the sense of individuality or egoism; *buddhi*, intellectual or reasoning faculty, and *citta* or cognition. Judging by Yeats's description, *Passionate Body* seems to correspond to *manas*, *ahaṁkāra* and *citta*.[75] *Ahaṁkāra* is the principle that creates the sense of personality. It is the principle of individual consciousness in its possessive aspect:

> Having received every kind of knowledge, action, decision and experience from the intellect, it puts a stamp of 'mineness' upon their impressions, deposits them in the *citta* and exhibits them to Purusa, the soul.[76]

When Yeats says of *Passionate Body* that it is "images that we associate with ourselves"[77] he is referring to the possessive aspect of sensation and perception. He noted that according to the automatic script "sensuous" was defined in an unexpected way. "An object is sensuous if I relate it to myself, 'my fire, my chair, my sensation'...."[78] In its objective aspect *Passionate Body* refers to all created objects, light, nature; it also includes all men and women that an individual is linked to by passion, those whom he likes or dislikes, loves or hates. "When we perceive the *Daimons* as *Passionate Body*, they are subject to time and space, cause and effect...."[79]

Yeats does not distinguish very sharply between *Spirit* and *Celestial Body*; according to him they are mind and its object. *Celestial Body* is "the Divine Ideas in their unity," therefore it can be seen as *vijñānamaya kośa* or the sheath of intellect. *Spirit* according to Yeats is the *Daimon*'s knowledge, for "in the *Spirit* it knows all other *Daimons* as the Divine Ideas in their unity."[80] *Spirit* seems to correspond most to *buddhi* or reason, the discriminative principle. Yeats defined *buddhi* in his essay on the *Māṇḍūkya Upaniṣad*: "*Buddhi* is described as that which 'distinguishes' between *Tamas, Rajas, Satva,* that it may cling to *Satva*, but 'distinguishes' suggests Discursive Mind; perhaps it instantly recognises and clings."[81] It is reason that helps man to discriminate between real and unreal, self and not-self, and to understand truth: "pure mind, containing within itself pure truth..."[82]

The *Principles* inform the *Faculties* and it is the *Faculties* alone that operate in life. When the *Principles* move from concave to convex, from a discarnate into an incarnate state, they become the *Faculties.*

Yeats describes the *Four Faculties* as the four memories of the *Daimon*.[83] The faculty corresponding to *Husk* is *Will*. It is the waking state, a state in which man identifies himself with his body. It indicates desires and aspirations of which the will is conscious, and actions done voluntarily, although these in turn result from past abilities inherited as instinct. It becomes normal ego or memory of present life.

To *Passionate Body* or the perceptive, imaginative mind correspond the objects of those desires. *Mask* is man's idea formed out of the deeply embedded memory of the moments of exaltation in his past life. *Mask* corresponds to the dreaming state in which mental forms of objects predominate. *Bṛhad-āraṇyaka Upaniṣad* describes the waking and dreaming states thus:

> Verily, there are just two states of this person (the state of being in) this world and the state of being in the other world.... When he goes to sleep he takes along the material of this all-embracing world, himself tears it apart, himself builds it up... There are no joys there... but he creates joys, pleasures and delights....He, indeed is the agent (maker or creator).[84]

In this context Yeats refers to the plot of Flaubert's story in which the waking and dreaming states oppose each other exactly as the Upaniṣad explains: it envisaged a man whose dreams grew in magnificence as his life grew increasingly unlucky.[85] Thus, *Mask* as memory of moments of exaltation determines man's image of the ideal.

To *Spirit* as knowledge corresponds the faculty of *Creative Mind*; it constitutes memory of ideas—or universals displayed by actual men in past lives. *Creative Mind* can also be understood as the state of dreamless sleep, a state in which pure consciousness exists without reference to subject or object. It is "Prajña, whose sphere (of activity) is the state of deep sleep..."[86] This is "knower" or *Creative Mind*, that contains memory of universals. These universals are the unchanging laws of nature. *Celestial Body* or Necessity creates *Body of Fate* or individual destiny. His *Body of Fate*, "the series of events forced upon him from without, is shaped out of the *Daimon*'s memory of the events of his past incarnations."[87]

The Upaniṣads regard man as a conscious complex whose constituent parts are body, senses, mind, intellect, and spirit. To these is added nescience, ignorance that spirit or self is its eternal component. The latter idea is supported in Yeats's statement: "that instant is of necessity unintelligible to all bound to the antinomies."[88] It is this nescience that impels man to act. Nescience is referred to in the Upaniṣads as *māyā* or *avidyā* and is the inexplicable effect of the creative power of God on the mind of man. Max Mueller explains that one aspect of nescience is "our inevitable ignorance of all that is transcendent," and awareness only of the phenomenal.[89] Its true position is relative, not absolute. At the end of 'Leda and the Swan,' Yeats asks the following question:

> Being so caught up,
> So mastered by the brute blood of the air,
> Did she put on his knowledge with his power
> Before the indifferent beak could let her drop?[90]

The answer to this is to be found in *A Vision* where Yeats says that ultimate reality falls in human consciousness into a series of antinomies, thesis and anti-thesis. "Knowledge and power" are indeed "put on" by Leda, or nature, because the intelligent principle pervades it, the only difference being that this knowledge is not absolute, but a knowledge of contradictions and antinomies. The thesis, for example, that nature exists because it appears tangible, seems as true as the anti-thesis that nature does not exist as it will disappear after a certain lapse of time. The search for absolute knowledge of nature is proved to be futile, as it results in opinion cancelled by counter-opinion. Radhakrishnan's comment is underlined by Yeats: "Things of the world are ever-changing their forms, and they cannot be considered real in an ultimate sense."[91] Nescience creates ego or *ahaṁkāra*, a possessive attitude towards the objects of the world, which appear to be real in an absolute sense. Yeats presents this attitude in the figure of Congal in *The Herne's Egg*. Congal does not believe in the existence of a Supreme Spirit underlying nature's phenomena. His attitude towards Attracta's faith in Him is derisive: "a woman thinks that she/ Is promised or married to a bird."[92] Congal is a symbolic figure representing *Passionate Body* in the macrocosm and ego or *ahaṁkāra* (the mind in its possessive, acquisitive aspect) in the microcosm. *Husk* and *Passionate Body* create a drive for fulfilment of desire; Congal advocates this attitude when he says to Attracta, "pick/ Or be picked by seven men."[93] Congal's desire for the eggs of the Herne displays the acquisitive attitude of the materialist. Pat, one of the characters in the play draws a distinction between Hernes and hens:

> What do hens eat? Hens live upon mash,
> Upon slop, upon kitchen odds and ends.
> What do hernes eat? Hernes live on eels,
> On things that must always run about.
> Man's a high animal and runs about… [94]

This verse appears modelled by Yeats upon the following lines from the *Kaṭha Upaniṣad*:

> The ignorant man runs after pleasure, sinks into the entanglements of death; but the wise man, seeking the undying, does not run among things that die[95]

and,

> As rain upon a mountain ridge runs down the slope, the man that has seen the shapes of Self runs after them everywhere.[96]

In terms of the play's symbolism a herne is a wise man who has realized his identity with the Herne or Spirit. The hen represents the ignorant man who seeks the "kitchen odds and ends" that symbolise the perishable nature of objects in the world. Congal, because of his ignorance, is termed a fool; he is ignorant of the great truth expressed in the *Īśa Upaniṣad*: "Whatever lives is full of the Lord. Claim nothing; enjoy, do not covet His property."[97]

When *Principles* and *Faculties* interact there is creation;[98] the force that impels man to act is the search for eternal, unchanging happiness; it causes him to form elaborate plans for achieving this happiness. When Yeats says that the *Faculties* find their unity in the *Mask,*[99] he means exactly this. The sheath of bliss is within man, but owing to ignorance of his true nature, man seeks it without. Explaining this urge in one of his earliest lectures, Mohini Chatterjee had said that the ultimate aim of all effort was the production of happiness. 'The author of the Upanishads shows great wisdom when he asks: "who would have moved or who would have lived if happiness did not pervade all space."'[100] As Yeats explains, all art, economics and science are the result of different varieties in the combination of *Principles* and *Faculties*. In the wheel of the *Faculties* he says, "*Will* predominates during the first quarter, *Mask* during the second, *Creative Mind* during the third, *Body of Fate* during the fourth."[101]

The idea expressed in Yeats's terminology finds simpler expression in the *Bṛhad-āraṇyaka Upaniṣad*:

> As is his desire; so is his will; as is his will, so is the deed he does, whatever deed he does, that he attains.[102]

Creative Mind in itself is devoid of matter; that is supplied by *Mask*; form is imparted to matter by *Creative Mind*. In proportion as *Will* is joined to universal or natural laws, one creates or materializes the imagined.

Yeats's basic premise as well as that of the Upaniṣads is man's freedom. According to the *Bṛhad-āraṇyaka Upaniṣad*, good actions lead to the formation of virtuous character, while evil acts result in evil character.[103] In the idealist theories of creation, the effect is merely a changed appearance and not a transformation of the cause.[104] It has been noted earlier that creation is merely an idea of the Creator. Yeats's poem, 'Leda and the Swan' also illustrates this philosophy. Leda's violent rape begets repeated violence, which is projected on to the historical scene. The Trojan war, the death of Agamemnon, is effect repeating cause, as in a mirror.

The relation between an act and its consequence is not dictated by an arbitrary determinism; Annie Besant had explained that there is not only a definite relation, but an "identity between the invisible and visible parts of every activity." An observed, invariable sequence is called a law of nature.[105] In the moral field this law is known as *karma*. Charles Johnston, in his *Karma*: *Works and Wisdom,* had explained that in the esoteric doctrine of the Upaniṣads, *karma* meant the mental and moral forces that led either to liberation, or to reincarnation.[106] That Yeats entirely agreed with this view is obvious from the following statement: "When *Passionate Body* predominates all is *Destiny*."[107] He referred to the Hermetic Fragments which maintain that destiny sows the seeds of events and impels evil men; he disagreed with their view, however, that "destiny inspires only evil men." He was in agreement with the Upanisadic doctrine that all action, whether good or evil, performed in a spirit of passionate attachment, bears good or evil fruit or destiny.

Thus every objective manifestation of evil (or good) in the present is a congealing of subjective desire in the past. Yeats learnt this truth from theosophical renderings of the Upaniṣads, and confirmed it through his own occult studies. He learnt that evil appeared a "problem" only as long as the essential nature of the self was not realized, that the self had the power to materialize every emotion or thought, and that *Body of Fate* was traceable to *Will*. He had recorded in 1909 that it was possible that emotion was an evocation and could alter events by creating good and evil luck. He elaborated that much hatred inevitably brought about violent events, and sometimes "an actual stream of ill luck." The same was true of other emotions embodied in nature symbols: "a meditation on sunlight for instance, affects the nature throughout, producing all the effects which follow from the symbolical nature of the sun."[108] Yeats was familiar with the Upanisadic law that subtle can become gross, a law based upon the power of will as a faculty of the soul. It was his faith that "everything we formulate in the imagination if we formulate it strongly enough, realises itself in the circumstances of life."[109] Yeats's mastery of these truths emerged in *A Vision* as the metaphysics of *Will* and *Body of Fate*.

A particular man is classified according to the place of will, or choice, in Yeats's diagram of the phases of the moon. This is again because there is a direct link between *Body of Fate* and *Will* or desire, the symbolism of the phases of the moon being a suitable way of indicating the various personalities that result from "desire and absence of desire." and the character and personality that result therefrom. The Yeatsian analogy between the moon and mind is age-old, and can be traced to the *Ṛg-Veda*. "The moon was produced from his mind," says the Ṛg-Vedic seer. The waxing and waning of the moon symbolizes the waxing and waning of desires in the mind, and its changes between light and dark indicate the alternating optimism and pessimism of the mind. In the *Bṛhad-āraṇyaka Upaniṣad,* we are told that "the mind, verily, is the organ of perception; it is seized by desire as an over-perceiver, for through the mind one desires desires."[110]

All incarnations, except those at phases one and fifteen, are governed by the law of rebirth, which is contingent upon desire as well as nescience, or apprehension of duality. According to the Upaniṣads, desire is the root of empirical existence. Yājñavalkya explains that "the object to which the mind is attached, the subtle self goes together with the deed, being attached to it alone."[111] The sensual desires that lead to death and rebirth are referred to in 'Sailing to Byzantium': "The young/ In one another's arms/ Those dying generations."[112] The world of nature comprises of "whatever is begotten, born and dies"; in 'Byzantium' it is referred to as "mere complexities,/ The fury and the mire of human veins."

However, there is no satisfaction after fulfilment of desire has taken place. This is because everything in nature is subject to change. In 'Nineteen Hundred and Nineteen,' Yeats spoke of "The circle of the moon/ That pitches common things about." However, "man is in love and loves what vanishes."[113] Yeats recognized that personality "is a constantly renewed choice."[114] When Congal says, "We all complete a task or circle,/ Want a woman, then all goes— pff,"[115] he expresses the idea that completion of a task brings only temporary fulfilment of desire, and man is ever planning a new task. This process continues till man exhausts the possibilities offered by nature and arrives at reality. This conflict between *Will, Mask, Creative Mind,* and *Body of Fate* continues until man discovers that fulfilment comes only from discovery of that Real which is not subject to change. Yeats speaks of this in 'The Wheel':

> Through winter-time we call on spring,
> And through the spring on summer call...
> Nor know that what disturbs our blood
> Is but its longing for the tomb.[116]

According to Yeats, the Daimon or the ultimate self of man leads him to "whatever among works not impossible is the most difficult." Yeats offers an interesting analogy of the Daimon who suffers with man in the same way as a "firm-souled" man would suffer with the woman he loves.[117]

As we have noted earlier, man, the body-senses-mind-spirit complex is barred from self-realization through nescience. But the possibility of the individual understanding his true nature cannot be ruled out for all time because his inner core is knowledge, pure consciousness or *Ātman.* Individuality or ego persists up to the moment that duality either of desire ("is" and "ought"), or of knowledge ("knower" and "known") persists. The moment ignorance is destroyed, individuality, the product of nescience remains no more.

A man may be born, says Yeats, several times at a particular phase, sometimes four times, before he has the strength to move on to the next phase.[118] Owing to the predominance of ignorance, man's progress towards self-realization is slow. Rebirth itself is ordained by nature in order that man, rebuffed by dissatisfaction in endless pursuit of desire, learns that he must seek his own true self and not the changing phenomena. Nature is not only a changing, fleeting entity but in another aspect, a positive, guiding force. Equipped with his *Four Principles* and *Four Faculties* man moves from the primary to the antithetical phases and finally to Unity of Being. Some ignorance, however, is essential to remain in nature, for the moment the being realizes the truth, he is liberated and goes "out of nature," to use the phrase from 'Sailing to Byzantium.' That is why Yeats speaks of phases one and fifteen as supernatural incarnations.[119] Nature is however a necessary stepping stone on the soul's journey towards the spiritual and the mystical, the synthesis of subject and object, Yeats's Unity of Being.

As noted earlier, Yeats was aware in the 1925 version of *A Vision* that there were some differences between neo-Platonic philosophy and that of his instructors. He was aware of two different views of nature, one, that it was an emanation from, and the other, that it was a reflection of the One. The 1937 version of *A Vision* shows his acceptance of the idealistic theory of creation as explained in the Upaniṣads; herein he made Robartes the protagonist of this theory, and Aherne the spokesman of the transformation theory.[120] To Robartes' question, "Have I proved that civilizations come to an end when they have given all their light like burned out wicks," Aherne says, "Or transformation." Robartes, as Yeats's spokesman, enunciates that "Life is no series of emanations from divine reason such as the Cabalists imagine, but an irrational bitterness, no orderly descent from level to level, no waterfall but a whirlpool, a gyre."[121] He says that the *Four Principles* of Plotinus imply a descent from *Principle* to *Principle*, a fall of water from ledge to ledge, whereas a system presenting the phenomenal world as irrational because it consists of unresolved antinomies, must be represented as always returning to the starting point.[122] It is obvious here that Robartes represents the idealistic theory of creation, whereas Aherne and the Cabalists offer the transformation theory. As noted above, according to the idealistic view, the effect is merely a changed appearance of the cause, which remains in an unchanged state, and is not itself modified by the effect. The Upaniṣads enunciate this in the following verse:

> The yon is fulness; fulness, this.
> From fulness, fulness doth proceed.
> Withdrawing fulness's fulness off,
> E'en fulness then itself remains.[123]

The transformation theory, on the other hand, holds that the effect is a transformation of the material cause, implying that the cause is consumed in giving birth to effect.[124] Materialist theories are based on this view, as they hold that all effects are inherent in nature, which is its own cause. Yeats defined his own view in the play *The Herne's Egg,* which is a satire against the materialist position. Congal, one of the characters in the play, denies that there is a higher power than the individual; according to him nature runs its own course: that he shall die a fool "is but natural,/ And needs no curse to bring it."[125] Congal thinks that he can escape punishment by putting an end to his own life, thus cheating the Herne (who has decreed the curse), but he does not know that *karma* persists and creates rebirth; Congal is helpless in the face of his own rebirth as a donkey! Yeats portrays the idea that the Supreme Spirit is the efficient as well as the material cause of nature. He declares his judgement of the materialist who believes that nature is its own cause; the holder of such a view is turned into a donkey in spite of all his exertions:

> All that trouble and nothing to show for it,
> Nothing but just another donkey.[126]

Attracta, like Leda, represents nature that derives its power from the spirit that pervades it:

> She lies there full of his might,
> His thunderbolts in her hand .[127]

Nature appears to be moving and movable in her own right, but this is as much an illusion as the movements of puppets or dolls upon wire. Nature exists and moves by virtue of the fact that it is impregnated by spirit:

> Agnes Her limbs grow rigid, she seems
> A doll upon a wire.
>
> Mary Her human life is gone

> And that is why she seems
> A doll upon a wire.[128]

Bereft of the power of the Creator, nature is a void. Yeats has demonstrated through the plot of *The Herne's Egg* that *Brahman* or *Spirit* is the "inner controller" of everything. This idea is expressed in the *Bṛhad-āraṇyaka Upaniṣad*: "He who dwells in the earth… who controls the earth from within, he is your self, the inner controller, the immortal."[129]

The element of contrivance in *The Herne's Egg* is evident in the stage direction: "All should be suggested, not painted realistically. Many men fighting with swords and shields, but sword and shield, shield and sword, never meet."[130] It is also obvious in the reference to "the moon of comic tradition;"[131] this element sustains the metaphor of an artificially constructed drama, conveying the idea of life as a drama with the Creator as its director and the various people as the *dramatis personae.* Yeats uses this dramatic technique to portray the concept of the inner controller, the *sūtrātman*, literally, one who holds the threads in his hands.[132]

In this play, Yeats has conveyed his view that life is a comedy at the expense of the non-believer, who denies the existence of a superior power working behind nature's phenomena, and believes consequently in the supremacy of individual will. It is possible to see that Yeats wholly accepted the Upanisadic position, and in doing so equipped himself to see the fallacies in the materialistic theories of Huxley, Tyndall and other positivists who held sway in his time. His acceptance of the idealistic view of the Upaniṣads is also expressed in the line:

> Natural and supernatural with the self-same ring are wed.[133]

Notes

[1] See *Autobiographies*, p.32.

[2] *Ibid.*, pp.59–64.

[3] *Ibid.*, p.89.

[4] *Ibid.*, p.92,

[5] *Ibid.*, p.78.

[6] See *Essays*, p.189.

[7] See *Lucifer* I, 1, 8. Madame Blavatsky started the journal in 1887. It was changed to *The Theosophical Review* in 1897 with volume XXI.

[8] See A.P. Sinnett, "The Invisible World," *Lucifer* I, 3, 187.

[9] See H.P. Blavatsky, *The Secret Doctrine* (London,1888), I, 671. Hence cited as *Secret Doctrine.*

[10] S. Radhakrishnan, tr., *The Bhagavad-Gītā* (London: George Allen and Unwin Ltd., 1948) II, 69. All quotations from *The Bhagavad-Gītā* are from this edition.

[11] H.P. Blavatsky, *Isis Unveiled* (London: 1877), I, xx. Hence cited as *Isis.*

[12] Charles Johnston, *From the Upanishads* (London: The Theosophical Publishing Society, 1896).

[13] See W.B. Yeats, *Where There is Nothing, Plays for an Irish Theatre*, vol.1 (London: A.H. Bullen, 1903).

[14] *The Unicorn From the Stars, Collected Plays*, p.329.

[15] Ellis and Yeats, *Blake* (London: Bernard Quaritch, 1893), p.317.

[16] See *Secret Doctrine*, I, 129–30. Madame Blavatsky explained further that "in Occult metaphysics there are, properly speaking, two 'ONES'—the One on the unreachable plane of Absoluteness and Infinity, on which no speculation is possible, and the Second 'One' on the plane of Emanations. The former can neither emanate nor be divided, as it is eternal, absolute, and immutable.

The Second, being, so to speak, the reflection of the first One (for it is the Logos, or Īśvara, in the Universe of Illusion), can do all this." See also Subba Row's explanation of the Vedantic idea in a footnote on p.130.

17 *Chāndogya Upaniṣad*, III, 19, 1.

18 "Occultism and Modern Science," *The Irish Theosophist*, I, 1 (1892), p.11.

19 *Chāndogya Upaniṣad*, VI.12. 1, 2.

20 *Mythologies*, pp.189, 190.

21 *Plays for an Irish Theatre*, p.129.

22 See *Vision* (A), p.176.

23 *W.B. Yeats and Sturge Moore*, p.131.

24 See Ralph Griffith, trans., *Hymns of the Ṛg Veda* (Varanasi: The Chowkhamba Sanskrit Series office, 1889; rpt. 1963), X. 129, 2–4. Hence cited as *Ṛg Veda.*

25 *Bṛhad- āraṇyaka Upaniṣad*, I. 4.1.

26 *Indian Philosophy*, I, 171.

27 *Vision* (B). The quotations in the ensuing discussion are from pp.187–193.

28 See *Ṛg Veda*, X. 82.7.

29 *Collected Plays*, p.323.

30 See *Bṛhad-āraṇyaka Upaniṣad*, I. 2.1.

31 *Ṛg Veda*, X. 72.4.

32 *Collected Plays*, p.677.

33 See B.R. Sharma, *The Concept of Ātman in the Principal Upaniṣads* (New Delhi: Dinesh Publications, 1972), p.43: "Thus when the Vedic seer says, A is the father of B, he means to say that A produces B. But when he says, A is the child of B, he implies that when B produces something it produces nothing else but A. In brief, it should be said that B being produced by A,

when it produces something, reproduces A in a different mode. Thus this reciprocity is to show that the cause and the effect are the same in essence." Hence cited as *Concept of Ātman.*

34 See *Bṛhad- āraṇyaka Upaniṣad*, I. IV.3.

35 *Ibid.*, I. IV.7.

36 *Collected Poems*, p.328.

37 *Ibid.*, p.331.

38 See *Ṛg Veda*, X, 129.

39 *Ibid.*, I.10, 72.

40 *Bṛhad- āraṇyaka Upaniṣad*, IV.3.11.

41 See *Ṛg Veda*, IV. 40.5.

42 *Collected Plays*, p.645.

43 *Ibid.*, p.677. Also, Attracta refers to the Herne as the "unbegotten." *Ibid.*, p.650.

44 *Vision* (B), p.187; see Yeats's footnote.

45 *Collected Plays*, p. 650.

46 See *Vision* (B), p.67.

47 *Muṇḍaka Upaniṣad*, I. 1.7.

48 Purohit Swāmi's talk delivered at Madras University: "Philosophy of the Upaniṣads" (August 13, 1938), Swāmi Ms.

49 See *Vision* (B), p.33.

50 *Bṛhad- āraṇyaka Upaniṣad*, I. 4.2, 3.

51 *Vision* (B), p. 189.

52 *Collected Plays*, p. 653.

53 *Ibid.*, p.655.

54 See Yeats and Swāmi, p. 136: "He wanted every form, for He wanted to show Himself; as a magician He appears in many forms, He masters hundreds and thousands of powers."

[55] See *Concept of Ātman*, p.229.

[56] *Vision* (B), p.219.

[57] *Ibid*., p.67.

[58] *Bṛhad-āraṇyaka Upaniṣad*, IV. 4.20.

[59] *Taittirīya Upaniṣad*, II. 1.1.

[60] *Vision* (B), p. 193.

[61] 'The Philosophy of the Upaniṣads,' *Indian Philosophy*, I, 172.

[62] *Ibid*., p.161.

[63] See *Bṛhad-āraṇyaka Upaniṣad*, IV. 4.5.

[64] See *Kaṭha Upaniṣad*, I. 3.10.

[65] 'The Completed Symbol,' *Vision* (B), pp.187-92.

[66] See *Taittirīya Upaniṣad*, II.2.1–II.7.1 and III.1.1–III.6.1. Also see Appendix.

[67] See *Vision* (B), p. 188.

[68] See *Bṛhad-āraṇyaka Upaniṣad*, IV.4.3–5; the quotation from *Viṣṇu Smṛiti* is on p.116.

[69] See *Aitareya Upaniṣad*, I.2.4.

[70] *Vision* (B) p.191.

[71] See Annie Besant, *Reincarnation and Karma* (rpt. London: The Theosophical Society in England, 1965), p.20.

[72] V.S. Apte, *Students Sanskrit-English Dictionary* (Delhi: Motilal Banarsidass, 1890), p.573, defines *saṁskāra* as "impression on the memory, effect of work." Hence cited as Apte.

[73] (a) See *Vision* (B), p.191.

(b) See Apte, p.573.

[74] *Vision* (B), p.191.

[75] See *Yajurveda Saṁhita*, ed. Damodara Satavatekara (Paradi, 1957), VI.3.

76 Shri Swami Vyas Dev Ji Maharaj, *Science of Soul* (Rishikesh: Yoga Niketan Trust, 1964; rpt. 1977), p.97.

77 *Vision* (B), p. 188.

78 *Ibid.*, p.87.

79 *Ibid.*, p.189.

80 *Ibid.*

81 (a) *Essays*, p.482.

(b) See *Indian Philosophy*, I, 165. "Vijnana" written by Yeats in the margin of his copy.

82 See *Vision* (B), p.189.

83 *Vision* (B), p.83.

84 (a) *Bṛhad- āraṇyaka Upaniṣad*, IV.3.9, 10.

(b) See *Vision* (B), p.220.

85 See *Vision* (B), p.70.

86 *Māṇḍūkya Upaniṣad*, 11.

87 *Vision* (B), p. 83.

88 (a) *Ibid.*, p. 193.

(b) See also D.M. Datta, *The Six Ways of Knowing* (Calcutta: The University of Calcutta, 1960), p. 49: "It is under the stress of this *ajñāna* that *ātman* assumes an objective attitude. Assumption of the objective attitude directly leads to its further self-limitation. It creates a breach in the one whole of *caitanya*, a dualism of the self and the not-self, the subject and the object."

89 See Max Mueller, *Three Lectures on the Vedānta Philosophy* (London: Longman's Green and Co., 1901), p.97.

90 *Collected Poems*, p. 241.

91 *Indian Philosophy*, p.164 in Yeats's copy.

92 *Collected Plays*, p.749.

[93] *Ibid.*, p.650.

[94] *Ibid.*, p. 659.

[95] Yeats and Swāmi, p.33.

[96] *Ibid.*, p.34.

[97] *Ibid.*, p.15.

[98] See *Vision* (B), p.195.

[99] *Ibid.*, p.188.

[100] *Transactions of the London Lodge*, No.3, p.4.

[101] *Vision* (B), p. 192.

[102] *Bṛhad- āraṇyaka Upaniṣad*, IV.4.5.

[103] *Ibid.*, IV.4.5.

[104] See Chandradhar Sharma, *A Critical Survey of Indian Philosophy* (Delhi: Motilal Banarsidass, 1960), p.151. Hence cited as *A Critical Survey.*

[105] See Annie Besant, *Popular Lectures in Theosophy* (Ạdyar: The Theosophical Publishing House, 1910; rpt. 1938), p.97.

[106] See Charles Johnston, *Karma: Works and Wisdom* (New York: The Metaphysical Publishing Co., 1900), p.15. Hence cited as *Works and Wisdom.*

[107] *Vision* (B), p.190.

[108] *Autobiographies*, p.486.

[109] See Yeats's article, "Is the Order of R.R. & A.C. to Remain a Magical Order?" in *Golden Dawn*, p.265.

[110] *Bṛhad-āraṇyaka Upaniṣad*, III.2.7.

[111] *Ibid.*, IV.4.6.

[112] *Collected Poems*, p.217.

[113] *Ibid.*, p.232.

[114] *Vision* (B), p.84.

115 *Collected Plays*, p.661.

116 *Collected Poems*, p.237.

117 See *Mythologies*, p.361.

118 *Vision* (B), p.86.

119 *Ibid.*, p.183.

120 *Ibid.*, p.50.

121 (a) *Ibid.*, p.40.

(b) Yeats wrote to Dorothy Wellesley on July 26, 1939: "I have for years been creating a group of strange, disorderly people on whom Michael Robartes confers the wisdom of the east." *Letters*, p. 859.

122 See *Vision* (B), pp.194–195.

123 (a) See Hume, p.149. This verse is marked in Yeats's copy.

(b) See "Philosophy of the Upaniṣads," Swāmi Ms. Purohit Swāmi quoted the above verse from the *Īśa Upaniṣad* and explained: "Spirit the cause, Matter the effect, both cause and effect are perfect."

(c) Radhakrishnan explains in *The Principal Upaniṣads* that "the manifestation of this world does not take away from the fullness or integrity of the Absolute." See p.289.

124 See *A Critical Survey*, p.151.

125 *Collected Plays*, p.652.

126 *Ibid.*, p.678.

127 *Ibid.*, p.655.

128 *Ibid.*, p.654.

129 *Bṛhad-āraṇyaka Upaniṣad*, III.7.3.

130 *Collected Plays*, p.645.

131 *Ibid.*, p.671.

132 See Radhakrishnan: "Man is a bead strung on the thread of the

conscious self, and just as wooden puppets are worked by strings, so the world is operated by the *sūtrātman*, the thread spirit." *The Principal Upaniṣads*, p.225.

133 *Collected Poems*, p.328.

Chapter Three

Death and Immortality

> "Men dance on deathless feet"
>
> — 'Mohini Chatterjee'

Yeats devoted much effort and time to prove the immortality of the soul. Nature and human life were ever fleeting, ever changing; only a study of eschatology could reveal an unchanging substratum if one existed. To prove that the being continued to exist after death in some shape and form was to affirm immortality, to demonstrate that change itself was rooted in the unchanging. It is interesting to note that Yeats asserts the immortality of the soul in a context that presents death. In 'The Soul in Judgement' he refers to Paul Valéry contemplating a picture of the seaside cemetery and joyously concluding that human life must pass; Yeats then contrasts it with the prayer of the girl who sings: "O Lord, let something remain." He comments:

> I am convinced that the Upanishads—somebody had already given her the Pyramids—were addressed to the girl.[1]

According to him, the perennial yearning for immortality is not to be interpreted as a groping in the dark or wishful thinking, but rather as an intuitive apprehension of the reality that man is indeed immortal. Yeats rejects Paul Valéry and accepts the view of the Upaniṣads.

In the Upaniṣads too the teaching regarding the immortality of the soul is presented at many places in the context of death. For instance, in the *Bṛhad-āraṇyaka Upaniṣad*, Yājñavalkya asks Janaka:

"Where will you go when you are released (from this body)?"[2] Janaka, like many other initiates in various Upaniṣads, does not know the answer. In the *Chāndogya Upaniṣad* Śvetketu, upon affirming that he is properly instructed, is similarly asked: "Do you know to what place men go from here? Do you know how they return again?...do you know where the paths leading to the gods and leading to the fathers separate?"[3] When he replies negatively to these questions it is time for instructing him fully. The most dramatic of the Upaniṣads in this regard is the *Kaṭha Upaniṣad*, wherein Naciketas, desirous of obtaining the right answers chooses the Lord of death or Yama as his instructor.[4] Knowledge of eschatology is reserved as the final knowledge imparted to neophytes in the Upaniṣads. It is not regarded as satisfying any kind of morbid curiosity, but as complementary to knowledge of life, especially of liberation.

Yeats himself avidly sought the sort of knowledge that Naciketas yearned for. In the early stages of his enquiry he was more concerned about proving scientifically the immortality of the soul; it was only later, while revising *A Vision* that he became interested in liberation. Yeats's study of folklore, his experiments at séances and his avid interest in the proceedings of the Society for Psychical Research were aimed at confirming the basic premise that the soul was immortal. On this premise rested his belief in art, in civilizations, as immortality alone could ensure tradition. Yeats's desire to know more about death was sharpened by his own clairvoyant sensibilities as well as by the beliefs of those among whom he lived. In *Autobiographies* he mentions hearing some dead smuggler giving his accustomed signal.[5] In 'A General Introduction for My Work' he records that he heard in Sligo cottages or from Pilots at Rosses Point, many stories of apparitions of the recent dead or of legendary figures.[6]

As a young man he read manuals published by The Theosophical Society and *Esoteric Buddhism*. The author of *Hints on Esoteric Theosophy* referred to the adepts who "not only knew all about death, but were able to, and habitually did, watch the progress of the immortal portion of man after death," and knew what occurred and why.[7] Sinnett described the after-death states at some length in *Esoteric Buddhism*.[8] He claimed that his book contained the oriental doctrine regarding "the Science of Spiritual Causes and their Effects, of Super-Physical Consciousness, of Cosmical Evolution."

Yeats joined the Esoteric Section of the Theosophical Society in 1888 and was soon conducting occult experiments. However, he was asked to resign from the Society as he was "causing disquiet."[9] The real reason, however, was that Yeats longed for the kind of evidence that could be gained only through sīances, while the theosophists discouraged this kind of activity owing to their belief that it retarded the spiritual progress of the departed soul.[10]

Meanwhile he had been gathering more information on this head from stories read at the British Museum. These stories were compiled by him into anthologies,[11] the process obviously enabling him to study extra-terrestrial or post-mortem existence. In 1888 he had published *Fairy and Folk Tales of the Irish Peasantry* recording in his introduction that Irish belief in phantoms was age old and was unshaken by fashionable scepticism.[12] Yeats was sure that even a newspaper man, if enticed into a cemetery would believe in phantoms, "for everyone is a visionary if you scratch him deep enough. But the Celt is a visionary without scratching." He published other anthologies on the same theme: *Stories from Carleton* in 1889, *Irish Fairy Tales* in 1892, and *The Celtic Twilight* in 1893.[13]

In *Fairy and Folk Tales of the Irish Peasantry* he offered no theory: "The reader will perhaps wonder that I have not rationalized a single hobgoblin"; he agreed with Socrates' attitude of accepting the common opinion.[14] When he wrote 'Enchanted Woods' in 1902 he had come to believe that all nature was full of invisible beings ranging from the ugly and grotesque to the wicked.[15] He accompanied Lady Gregory when she went about the cottages of the Irish peasantry collecting similar tales. His own writings as well as his notes to Lady Gregory's *Visions and Beliefs in the West of Ireland*[16] reveal the many questions that arose in his mind regarding the nature of these apparitions.

His researches into folk-lore and his own ability to evoke visions using symbols and methods learnt at the Golden Dawn, stimulated belief in the actual existence of spirits, but his contact with the Society for Psychical Research created a sceptical attitude which even the Golden Dawn philosophy was inadequate to dispel! The Society did not believe in the "objective" existence of spirits as souls of the dead but regarded spirit or vision as "a symbolic event expressing a psychological state."[17] His self-contradictory responses to Maud

Gonne's questions regarding rebirth illustrate the case in point. His friend, George Russell, affirmed his belief in reincarnation but Yeats's immediate reaction was sceptical: "The whole doctrine of the reincarnation of the soul is hypothetical. It is the most plausible of the explanations of the world, but can we say more than that?"[18] However, when Maud Gonne spoke of an apparition that had appeared to her in childhood, his response was different. Accordingly, using the symbols of the Golden Dawn he evoked the spirit.[19] When the apparition became visible to Maud Gonne, while Yeats saw just a vague impression on the mind, he considered two alternatives. His initial reaction was to treat the apparition as the Society for Psychical Research would have done, that is, as an event symbolising a psychological state, but he remembered being taught at his initiation into the Esoteric Section of the Theosophical Society, that such a separated spirit "might haunt the soul in its new life and seek a reunion that must be refused."[20]

It was when Lady Gregory asked him to annotate her *Visions and Beliefs*, that he began an investigation of contemporary spiritualism and for several years frequented mediums who instructed the people upon their relations to the dead. He wrote to George Russell in 1898 saying that "he would like to know too what death looks like when they see it in the air."[21] Then he compared evidence gathered in folklore and séance with Swedenborg as well as with Indian belief.[22]

His notes to *Visions and Beliefs*[23] indicate the comparative nature of his researches; he referred to Madame Blavatsky, Swedenborg, and Henry More. But the general tenor of his notes indicates that he was not prepared to accept as final any of these views on the nature of apparitions or visions. Madame Blavatsky represented Indian thought: *akāśa*, she explained as an Indian word for astral light. Yeats, however, felt that the Indian theory of *akāśa* and the corresponding Western theory of astral pictures indicated the despair of some visionary to express a more metaphysical idea. Swedenborg's theory that when we die we live over again the events that are in our memory, he found more acceptable. He was full of other questions: was the soul itself memory? The theory he found most comprehensible at this stage was that shared by Madame Blavatsky and Shelley, who both believed in "a memory of nature distinguished from individual memory, though including and enclosing it."

His notes to *Visions and Beliefs*, his essays 'Swedenborg, Mediums and the Desolate Places' and 'Per Amica Silentia Lunae' reveal that he delved deeply into both Eastern and Western writers, who sought to explain the doctrine of the immortality of the soul.[24] Among Indian writings available to him were not only Madame Blavatsky's *The Secret Doctrine* but also a number of translations of the Upaniṣads, as well as some very lucid writing dealing with the subject of eschatology and immortality as presented by the seers of the Upaniṣads. In *Transactions of the London Lodge of the Theosophical Society* there is a record of a meeting held on 11 June 1884, in which Mohini Chatterjee answered many questions regarding *karma* and justice in the context of rebirth.[25] In another "open meeting" held on 10 December 1884, he read a paper, "On the Higher Aspect of Theosophic Studies"[26] in which he asserted that the soul was immortal though it passed through many births. The entire paper was based on the view of the Upaniṣads that change, visible as incarnation, birth, life and death, had an unchanging substratum. *Īśa Upaniṣad* had affirmed this truth:

> (Know that) all this, whatever moves in this moving world, is enveloped by God. [27]

The seer had sought to explain that the Supreme could be comprehended only as the inexplicable union of an eternal immutability and an unceasing change. This principle manifested itself in human life also.

During the 1890s Yeats became familiar with a great deal of literature dealing with the themes of death and rebirth. In *From the Upanishads* (1896) Charles Johnston referred to the story of Yama and Naciketas from the *Kaṭha Upaniṣad*; Yama or death was "our sincerest friend" since he taught us "what no other can—the lesson of the full and ever present eternity of life."[28] Charles Johnston published in 1899 *The Memory of Past Births* (a work based on Madame Blavatsky's 'Fragments of Truth' published earlier in *The Theosophist*).[29] He explained the "solar" and the "lunar" paths mentioned in the Upaniṣads as the eschatological spiritual and psychic states in which the souls of the dead found themselves. In 1900 he published *Karma: Works and Wisdom*, explaining in a chapter entitled

'Karma in the Upaniṣads,' that the Upanisadic doctrine embraces the "whole doctrine of Reincarnation, Karma and Liberation—the complete esoteric philosophy of India."[30]

In *A Vision* (1925), Yeats referred to a work by "some learned Indian" recommended to him by Florence Farr that described the soul's journey, "how it is whirled about/wherever the orbit of the moon can reach/until it plunge into the sun...."[31] The folklore belief in immortality he confirmed by his own researches into spiritualism. He noted in his *Memoirs*: "Have now proved spirit identity—for the ER case is final."[32] The Upaniṣads confirmed most of his conclusions, providing a complete and satisfying explanatory basis for these; they also imparted the validity of tradition to his own findings. Yeats realized that folklore was a mythologized version of ancient metaphysical truths: "if Lady Gregory had not said when we passed an old man in the woods, 'That man may know the secret of the ages,' I might never have talked with Shri Purohit Swāmi nor made him translate his Master's travels in Tibet, nor helped him translate the Upanishads."[33] This fact was entirely borne out by the parallels between Irish folklore and the doctrines of the Upaniṣads.

One of the first things he had learnt from his study of folklore was the continuity of existence through alternating incarnate and discarnate states. In fact *The Celtic Twilight* was a collection of evidence that spirits often appeared to fulfill some obligation, to revenge a wrong, or simply to act as good genius to people. The Upaniṣads explained that the continuity between life and death was to be understood through the symbolism of waking and dreaming, of day and night. Yeats noted in *A Vision*:

> Certain Upanishads describe three states of the soul, that of waking, that of dreaming, that of dreamless sleep, and say man passes from waking through dreaming to dreamless sleep every night and when he dies.[34]

This idea is presented in the *Bṛhad-āraṇyaka Upaniṣad* wherein it is said that the being moves alone in the waking and dream states in this world and the next.[35] Yeats comments that this ancient analogy between a separated spirit or phantom and a dream of the night, was once a universal belief as he found it in all his investigations, in Irish literature and folklore, in Japanese plays, in Swedenborg, in the phenomena of spiritualism.[36] In *A Vision* he gave examples of Japanese, Aran and Indian ghosts to illustrate the point that death was merely an extension, a dreamlike continuation of life seen as the waking state.[37]

Yeats wrote in 'Anima Mundi' that there were two realities, "the terrestrial and the condition of fire."[38] The terrestrial condition was one of power, of evil, of the strain of opposites, while "in the condition of fire all is music and all rest." To this he added Henry More's belief that those who after repeated lives failed to find the rhythmic body or the "Condition of Fire," were born again.[39]

The Upaniṣads contained the parallel symbolism of the paths of the sun and the moon, also referred to as the path of the gods and the path of the fathers. Eschatological states also belonged to the bright or dark fortnights according as they led to the sun or the moon. In his introduction to *The Holy Mountain* Yeats summed up his understanding of the two paths. Those who have realized their unity with Brahma reach the Gods, who are symbolised as the senses, while others go to the blessed spirits of their fathers; for the latter there was no escape.[40] Various Upaniṣads refer to these paths; among them are *Bṛhad-āraṇyaka, Chāndogya, Kaṭha and Praśna*. *Bṛhad-āraṇyaka Upaniṣad*, for instance, has this to say about the bright fortnight:

> . . . those too who meditate with faith in the forest on the truth, pass into the light, from the light into the day, from the day into the half month of the waxing moon . . . In those worlds of Brahmā they live for long periods. Of these there is no return.[41]

Against this is the eschatological state of those who belong to the dark fortnight:

> But those who by sacrificial offerings, charity and austerity conquer the worlds, they pass into the smoke, from the smoke into the night, from the night into the half month of the waning moon. . . .[42]

These are born again on earth. These two conditions of the souls are to be understood in the context of the broad division of all existence into spirit and matter. The *Praśna Upaniṣad* explains that the Lord of Creation produces "the pair, matter and life."[43] In the Upaniṣads, fire and sun are seen as the symbols of Spirit or the Creator, and moon is the symbol of creation. *Kaṭha Upaniṣad* explains that the one Self is like fire; it assumes the shape of the object it enters.[44] The path of the sun is the one taken by the man who identifies himself with spiritual consciousness, with the light of the *Ātman*, whereas the path of the moon is for one who identifies himself with the passing forms that are illumined by that light. Fire or solar light is freedom, enlightenment; matter (the "terrestrial condition" mentioned in 'Anima Mundi'), is lunar light, bondage to objects of creation.[45] Those who meditate on the self are seen symbolically as being on the path of the sun. *Praśna Upaniṣad* says that they have realised the final destiny of the soul, therefore they are not reborn. On the other hand, the path of the ancestors is taken by one whose acts are performed with selfish desires, so the fulfillment of desires necessitates many births.

The same symbolism pervades Yeats's work, particularly books II and III of *A Vision* (1937). The midday light symbolises the changeless absolute and its reflection in the sea is the created world, or "*ouvrages purs d'une eternelle cause.*"[46] Before considering Yeats's eschatology it is necessary to refer briefly to the *Four Principles* (discussed in detail in the chapter of Nature). In the cone of the *Principles* the solar cone was light and the lunar dark, but their light was thought not nature. In the lunar cone, however, light was nature, the light of the faculties, of sensation.[47]

Yeats's studies on the path of the sun helped him to formulate his concept of Unity of Being, while his interest in the path of the moon illumined his researches into eschatology and rebirth. In the macrocosm, *Husk* and *Passionate Body* correspond to matter or nature, the path of ancestors or lunar light. The *Passionate Body* is referred to as the present, creation, light, the objects of sense. It is the created world and implies objects in the world most desired or possessed by an individual. *Passionate Body* is also the totality of those Daimons with whom the individual (or Daimon) seeks to come into contact; as seen earlier, the Daimons seen as *Passionate Body* are subject to time and space, cause and effect. (This is so because everything in nature is subject to cause and effect.) The Daimons, as long as they are treated by each other as separate individuals, act and react with each other till all bonds created among them in various lives have been exhausted and they see themselves as part of a unity. Existence in life as in death has for its purpose the achievement of this unity.

The Upaniṣads maintain that the gross body is the instrument for the attainment of liberation. It does this as it is endowed with senses and faculties which enable it to come into contact with other individuals. Liberation is the realization of spiritual identity with them, which in turn is a long process spreading over many lifetimes. Yeats accepts this view. When the being sees them as objects of sense, *Passionate Body* predominates and there is *Destiny*;[48] in other words, passion or attachment brings with it the inevitability of destiny. (Mohini Chatterjee had also explained that until we removed all desire from our acts they would necessitate reincarnation.[49]) The earlier idea that men were "a bundle of cords knotted together"[50] Yeats was now able to understand more fully; these were the "knots" of passion that prevent Unity of Being and must be expiated after death or in another life.[51]

Yeats says that the *Principles* are relevant while discussing life after death. *Husk* is the physical body during life, and after death its record. This corresponds to the sheath of the body in the Upaniṣads (*annamaya kośa*). *Passionate Body* is described in *A Vision* as images that we associate with ourselves. It is the sheath of mind in its aspect of desire and attachment. *Spirit* he describes in the first version of *A Vision* as abstract mind for it has life only when united to the *Passionate Body* or *Celestial Body*.[52] He gives a more detailed description of it in the later version of *A Vision* where he states that when it was attached to *Passionate Body* it was a record of all actions and thoughts of the individual extending over many lifetimes.[53]

At death consciousness passes from *Husk* to *Spirit*; *Husk* and *Passionate Body* are said to disappear "which corresponds to the enforcing of *Will* and *Mask* after phase 22; as in the primary phases, *Creative Mind* clings to *Body of Fate*."[54] The last primary phases of a closing lunar cycle are symbolic both of liberation and of death; in life they stand for the attention of personality, acceptance of fate or the will of God, and in death for the literal disappearance of personality that takes place. Phase 22 has already been defined as one in which the being so uses the intellect that the last vestige of personality disappears.[55] *Will* submitting to *Body of Fate* is a spiritual experience in life, whereas in death it is to be taken literally, as the being has no control over death as fate. *Spirit* turns away from *Passionate Body* and turns to *Celestial Body*.[56] This again is true of both states; in the state of liberation Spirit or mind turns away from *Passionate Body* or objects of desire, towards *Celestial Body* or divine ideas; in death *Husk* and *Passionate Body* vanish as active faculties but merge into *Spirit* as *Principles*. *Bṛhad-āraṇyaka Upaniṣad* explains that all the faculties merge into the self at the time of death:

> Just as policemen, magistrates, chariot drivers, leaders of the village gather round a King who is departing, even so do all the breaths (senses) gather round the self at the end.[57]

Bṛhad-āraṇyaka Upaniṣad explains that at the moment of death he becomes one with intelligence. His knowledge, work, and past experience depart with him.[58] The unit consisting of the senses (in their subtle form as faculties), mind with its impressions of the past and its knowledge, along with the vital breath is known as the subtle body or *sūkśma śarira*. At death this unit "is lit up by the subjective aspect, i.e. by the all-pervasive consciousness, *Ātman*."[59]

In Yeats's terminology this process is the absorption of the *Faculties* into the *Principles*, the movement from the "convex" or incarnate state into the "concave" or discarnate state. As the subtle body quits the *Husk* or physical body, it takes along with it *karma* or record of actions done in life, which merges with the record of the individual soul referred to by Yeats as the Daimon or *Ghostly Self*. This is the *Record* where the images of all past events remain always, the idea that Yeats was familiar with in theosophy and popular mysticism as "pictures in the astral light." Thus in the concept of "record" corresponding to the concept of *karma* as impressions of actions recorded in memory (referred to as *saṁskāra*) in the Upaniṣads, Yeats finally found an answer to his questions regarding pictures in the astral light. As already mentioned, Yeats had said in his notes to *Vision and Beliefs* that this idea (of astral pictures) came from the despair or some visionary to find a more metaphysical theory. Yeats's acceptance of the *karma* theory forms, as in the Upaniṣads, the basis of all other theories regarding the journey of the soul. The question regarding death in the Upaniṣads is "What then becomes of the person?"[60] Yeats wrote the meaning of this sentence in the margin of his copy of Hume: "Who then does the person become" and also marked the answer that followed:

> What they said was *karma* (action). What they praised was *karma*. Verily, one becomes good by good action, bad by bad action.

The "subtle body" of the Upaniṣads is Yeats's *Celestial Body*. When he says in 'Book II: The Completed Symbol' that "*Celestial Body* is said to age," he means that the subtle body gathers the impressions of deeds through countless incarnations. The ageing is not in physical terms but in terms of experience that is gathered through successive lives. These impressions are exhausted in the periods between lives as well as in many lifetimes. "Sometimes, grown old, it becomes the personification of evil," continues Yeats; this indicates that only evil deeds and their impressions are accumulated and as a result the individual soul or Daimon suffers in life after life. Yeats says in the footnote that perhaps his instructors drew upon some explanation of the lunar circuit, obliquely indicating a connection with the lunar symbolism of the Upaniṣads.[61]

In 'Book III: The Soul in Judgement' Yeats gives a detailed account of the after-death states of the soul, giving examples from folklore, learned authors, as well as from his first hand experience at sīances. The Upaniṣads however, do not go into details of the after-death states, nor do they give illustrations of specific cases. They do give, stated cryptically, certain unchanging laws that govern post-mortem experience and rebirth. They use chiefly the symbolism of the moon, of the dream state, and of the funereal and sacrificial fires, in order to make these laws comprehensible to the layman's imagination. However, it is remarkable that most of the conclusions reached by Yeats are identical with those of the Upaniṣads.

The first state is called *The Vision of the Blood Kindred* in which appear all persons related to the being through *Husk* and *Passionate Body*. According to Yeats, these apparitions become visible at the moment of dying and are part of the synthesis of "impulses and images" that takes place at death. We have already noted that the *Bṛhad-āraṇyaka Upaniṣad* refers to this synthesis, this coming together in the dying man of the predominant facts in his psyche:

> He is becoming one, he does not see, they say; he is becoming one, he does not smell . . . And when life thus departs, all the vital breaths depart after it. He becomes one with intelligence. (IV.4.2)

Yeats refers to the Indian who hated acting, as he believed that if a man died while acting Hamlet he would be Hamlet after death,[62] this is only a rendition in terms of folk belief, of the doctrine that a person's most powerful desires, or the desires finally synthesised by the mind, fructify in a future life. *Praśna Upaniṣad* clearly states "Whatever is one's thinking, therewith one enters into life."[63] *Chāndogya Upaniṣad* explains that on the basis of this doctrine of fashioning the desired sphere out of *saṁkalpa* or desire, the being sees his fathers, friends and those he wishes to see in the state ensuing death. The following verse is marked in Yeats's copy of *The Thirteen Principal Upanishads*:

> Of whatever object he becomes desirous, whatever desire he desires, merely out of his conception it arises. Possessed of it, he is happy.[64]

Sinnett had also explained that a person whose happiness or earth had consisted in the exercise of affections continued to live in the presence of those he loved: "For the person who loved them *they will* be there."[65] This state is followed by the *Meditation*. According to Yeats, the *Spirit* begins to understand its *Celestial Body* but needs the language and will of the incarnate. In the Upaniṣads too there is an occasional mention of the fact of possession. Patañcala's daughter was possessed by an aerial spirit, a *gandharva,* so she served as a medium.[66] The spirit imparted to the questioners information about their ancestors.

The second state is the *Dreaming Back*, which is from the being's *Passionate Body*; the *Spirit* is compelled to live over and over again the events that had most moved it. The Upaniṣads explain that in the dreaming state (in life as in death), the self remains awake and is aware of the impressions of deeds that are in the mind.[67] Mind lives in the deed till the experience is exhausted. Yeats says that into this category may be put apparitions that haunt the places where they have lived, that fill the literature of all countries and are the theme of Japanese Noh drama. The basic law in the Upaniṣads about subjective experience is that the place, object, or person to which the mind is attached by desire binds it—it lives subjectively in the same till that particular desire is exhausted, causing meanwhile bondage to space and time.[68] It is a physical law that sensation is only weakened by successive repetition.

To the *Dreaming Back* belonged apparitions of the murderer still dragging his victim, of the miser still counting his money, the pictures in the astral light. Yeats presents in *Purgatory* the souls that revisit familiar spots and "Re-live/Their transgressions, and that not once/ But many times…."[69] Speaking of the pictures in 1930 Yeats had noted that they showed arrested action: "we feel as if we could walk round it as if there was no fixed point of view."[70] He had asked his instructors, "whose perception do we share?" They replied that it was not a remembered perception, and left him to find an explanation. Yeats learnt from the Upaniṣads that these pictures were memory of the individual soul and were about his *karma*. It was not a subjective but a factual record since it contained all aspects of an act whether or not noticed by the mind of the being. It was not a remembered perception because it might belong to a life-time other than the present one. "That continuity is in the *Passionate Body* of the permanent Self or *Daimon*."[71] He presented this idea of arrested action, of "*Passionate Body* lifted out of time" in *The Death of Cuchulain* in a scene where Emer walks round representative figures of the killers of Cuchulain as if she saw the wounding in a trance and as if the killers were still there.[72]

A similar picture of memory, of *Passionate Body* preserved in the *Spirit* or impression in the mind (*saṁskara*) is described in *Purgatory* wherein the ghost seems to ride "Upon a gravelled avenue/ All grass to-day." As the Old Man explains, the scene has no objective reality. "And yet/ There's nothing leaning in the window/ But the impression upon my mother's mind;/ Being dead she is alone in her remorse."[73] The reason why the mother of the Old Man cannot escape from her repetitive dream is that she still finds pleasure in the act and her pleasure is greater than her remorse. The moment her pleasure wears out there will be knowledge and the dream will end.

This knowledge comes to the discarnate being in the state called the *Return*.[74] In this state, says Yeats, the *Spirit* under the influence of the *Celestial Body* lives through past events in the order of their occurrence so that each passionate event is traced to its source, until the sequence of events is understood in terms of cause and consequence. Thus suffering is understood as the result of certain forces released by the being himself. This knowledge creates a sense of justice and brings about equilibrium; it is a knot that is untied, an oscillation brought to a standstill. Yeats states in 'A Dialogue of Self and Soul,' that he does not wish to escape rebirth altogether. What he does wish for, however, is the knowledge that connects his past actions with their consequences, so that he can understand himself:

> I am content to follow to its source
> Every event in action or in thought;

> Measure the lot; forgive myself the lot![75]

Yeats believed that the more complete the *Dreaming Back* the more complete the *Return*. In other words, the greater the intensity with which the original act is re-lived, or the greater the suffering, the greater the clarity of self-knowledge and physical beauty. Yeats spoke of this in 'The Phases of the Moon':

> …though scarred
> As with the cat-o'-nine-tails of the mind,
> His body moulded from within this body
> Grows comelier.[76]

The impressions upon the mind bring both suffering and self-knowledge. Yeats expresses the same thought in *The Only Jealousy of Emer*, a play about spiritual knowledge gained through the process of death and rebirth: "How many centuries spent/ The sedentary soul…/ To raise into being/ That loveliness?"[77]

The next state is the *Phantasmagoria*, which exists to exhaust emotion. This state completes not only life, but also imagination. To this state belong spirits that are undergoing moral and emotional suffering. Disbelief or the kind of belief held in life determines the nature of suffering in this state. Yeats gives many examples of this state: a man who believed when living that death ends all may think of himself as a decaying corpse. He also mentions the instance of a girl in a Japanese play who is suffering because it seems to her "exaggerated conscience" that she has committed a great sin. The priest explains to her that the flames that surround her would vanish if she ceased to believe in them; this she cannot do as her belief is based upon a code held in life. In *The Celtic Twilight* Yeats had narrated many stories wherein disbelief in God leads to suffering. 'Village Ghosts' gives the example of a "misbeliever" who ventured to sleep in a haunted house and was flung out of the window along with his bed.[78] It is obvious here that the original idea of subjective suffering has undergone some transformation in the popular imagination. The Upaniṣads contain the basic formula that a man becomes what he knows, and that non-belief leads to non-existence.[79] As we have seen in the previous chapter, Yeats illustrated this idea in *The Herne's Egg* through the figure of Congal, whose lack of belief in the Herne as the Supreme Spirit, is responsible for turning him into a fool, a donkey. Yeats also states that a being assumes a shape suggested by the social or religious tradition of its past life. He gives the example of a spirit that appeared as a sheep with short legs and a decaying human head. Yeats interprets this as a symbolical state indicating a dying man, terrified that the body with which he identified himself would decay, and also suffering "an abject religious humility."[80] There is also a tale in 'Village Ghosts' about a man who haunted his own garden in the shape of a rabbit. *Īśa Upaniṣad* in a section entitled, 'The Denying Spirits', sets forth the following doctrine:

> Demoniac, verily, are those worlds enveloped in blinding darkness, and to them go after death, those people who are the slayers of the self.[81]

Mohini Chatterjee had explained that the worst sin was spiritual sin: "The worst of all is spiritual suicide; this occurs when a man denies that he has any spiritual nature and acts up to this belief." He had also asserted that one must not go against one's innermost divine self, "the Augoeides of the Greeks and the *Atma* of the Brahmins by self abasement," for that would be "the unpardonable sin, the sin against the Holy Ghost."[82]

Linked to this view is Yeats's idea that guilt or knowledge of wrong doing is its own punishment. Penance consists in the repeated dream, since that too brings suffering to the individual self. Yeats presented this idea very forcefully in *The Dreaming of the Bones* wherein Diarmuid and Dervorgilla who betrayed their country, relived their old lives after death. The Young Man in the play explains that for "an old scruple" they must suffer in various ways:

> I have heard that there are souls
> Who, having sinned after a monstrous fashion,
> Take on them, being dead, a monstrous image
> To drive the living, should they meet its face,
> Crazy, and be a terror to the dead.[83]

Yeats's play renders in dramatic terms the law of the Upaniṣads that according as one acts, according as one behaves, so does he become. At the end of this state which may last "with diminishing pain and joy for centuries," events are understood as cause and consequence and can be dismissed. Yeats holds the view that knowledge of cause and consequence is not enough; for complete justice the roles of victim and tyrant must be reversed; man's nature is reversed till a proper knowledge of good and evil is obtained. As far as the Upaniṣads are concerned, there are two points to be noted here. The first is that a man may suffer the consequences of his deeds in the dream state while beholding fearful sights, such as imagining that he is being killed or pursued by elephants.[84] The second point is that the Upaniṣads do not mention the reversal of roles as an eschatological stage. However, expiation takes place of necessity in subsequent lifetimes, as souls find rebirth according to their deeds and thoughts.[85] According to Yeats, the tyrant must of necessity become the victim, and the one who has been passive gets the power to control the other, "once tyrant, now victim."[86] He illustrated this in *The Herne's Egg* in Corney's conjecture that his donkey was a highway-man in his last birth: "What if before your present shape/ You could slit purses and break hearts,/ You are a donkey now, a chattel...."[87] Owing to a natural consequence of his *karma* a reversal of roles has taken place and in the present incarnation he is a taker, not giver of blows. The same law is illustrated in the case of Congal the King who must be reborn a donkey. The master becomes a slave or victim and vice versa.

When good and evil vanish into the whole there is a moment of consciousness called the *Marriage* or the *Beatitude*. This state comes after many births and deaths. The *Beatitude*, the *Purification*, and the *Foreknowledge* are not eschatological states according to the Upaniṣads, as there can be nothing new in death, which is a state of effects, not causes.[88] *Chāndogya Upaniṣad* explains (in a verse marked by Yeats in his copy) that knowledge must be achieved in life, it cannot be gained in death:

> Those who go hence without here having found the Soul (Ātman) and those real desires (*satya kāma*)—for them in all the worlds there is no freedom. But those who go hence having found here the Soul and those real desires—for them in all worlds there is freedom.[89]

These states of liberation correspond in the Upaniṣads to the path of the sun or of the gods, which in turn accords with Yeats's Unity of Being.

The great discovery of the seers of the Upaniṣads is that acts done with attachment or with a desire for results leave impressions in the mind, while those done with detachment, with a sense of duty, do not leave any mark.[90] Yeats has exactly the same view. The life of desire is Yeats's *Passionate Body*; it signifies the life of attachment to material objects as well as all relationships based on love, hatred, enmity and other emotions; the life of detachment is characterized by *Spirit* working as *buddhi* or discriminative faculty. The former creates destiny, Yeats's word for acts that bind, the latter is fate, or conduct illumined with the understanding of the true goal of human life, union with the Supreme. When *Passionate Body* predominates, the man acts in spite of reason, creating destiny; while he finds through reason or through the *Spirit* fate or Necessity.[91] *Passionate Body* creates the narrow, individual self with its exaggerated self-importance, desire for pleasure, and an acquisitive attitude. It is aptly illustrated in the character and destiny of Congal. In seeking to possess Attracta and trying to steal and enjoy the Herne's eggs, he typifies the possessive and acquisitive attitude of the materialist. Yeats's intention to show Congal turning into a fool and about to reincarnate as a donkey, may have been suggested by the following description of the ignorant man by Radhakrishnan:

> If instead of reason, our senses guide us, our life will be a mirror of passing passions and temporary inclinations. He who leads such a life will have to be written down, like Dogberry, an ass.[92]

Yeats says in 'The Soul in Judgement' that the monuments of the dead say to the poet that he is the light, but he is not persuaded:"The worm devours not only the dead, but as self-love, self-hate . . . devours the living also."[93] The worm that devours the living is this ignorance which results in attachment. In the *Kaṭha Upaniṣad* Yama, the lord of death, explains to Naciketas that bondage is caused by the good (*śreyas*) and the pleasant (*preyas*) alike.[94] "Pleasant" signifies not only pleasure-giving but also evil, as what is evil when done unto others appears pleasant to the doer. Yama means that acts performed with desire for personal gain leave their impressions in the mind (it is immaterial if those acts are good or evil), and cause bondage. Relationships based on affection and love must be lived in their fullness, and are exhausted in their natural course; those based on hatred and enmity must be expiated.As mentioned earlier, *Passionate Body* is the sum of those Daimons with whom such relationships have been formed. Sometimes the social code accepted by individuals prevents the fulfillment of a relationship, or else a single lifetime is insufficient for such fulfillment; thus a bond is created between them by unsatisfied desire.Yeats explains that any relation that is deeper than the intellect may become such a bond.[95] The story of John Bond and Mary Bell in 'Stories of Michael Robartes and His Friends' (section III) in *A Vision*, illustrates this very idea.When they met they fell in love at first sight. Both were "brought up in the strictest principles of the Church of Ireland;" Mary Bell was already married; these circumstances formed the social code that prevented their coming together. However, a residual memory of unfulfilled love creates a bond in their mind and they must meet at some point in time "accepting fate completely." Love, especially love at first sight, is the result of a bond formed in a previous life. "Those we have loved got their long fingers/ From death and wounds..." Death or non-requital of love may leave a relationship incomplete; for the sake of justice love must be returned in a future incarnation, the "long fingers" signifying the grip upon another of the one who has bestowed love previously. There are other bonds, memories of wrong done to others. Both Yeats and the seers of the Upaniṣads believe that these must be expiated during life; these form man's *Body of Fate*, the set of circumstances into which he is born. According to Yeats, the being must expiate between lives the ignorance that made them possible.

Yeats studied the whole question of crime and consequence not only on the level of personal relationships, but also in a larger social and national context. He said in the introduction to *The Words Upon the Window-Pane*: "I collect materials for my thought and work, for some identification of my beliefs with the nation itself...."[96] In his plays he presented acts that were wrong, not only because they were the result of blind passion, but also because they were wrongs done against class, society, or nation. In *The Dreaming of the Bones* he presents the idea that the crime of Diarmuid is not only blind passion but also its consequence, the betrayal of a nation:

> And for her sake and for his own, being blind
> And bitter and bitterly in love, he brought
> A foreign army from across the sea

and "sold their country into slavery."[97] The consequence is grievous since it has entailed the ruin of beautiful houses it had taken generations to build: "The enemy has toppled roof and gable,/ And torn the panelling from ancient rooms;/ What generations of old men had known/ Like their own hands..."[98]

In *Purgatory*, the mother of the Old Man acted in passion when she married the groom in a training stable, her sensuality symbolized by the tree with "leaves thick as butter,/ Fat, greasy life."[99] She did not foresee that she wronged not only herself but also her family and nation. The man she married was not of her class and in drunken stupor burnt down the ancient house. It was only in her after-death states of *Dreaming Back* and *Return* that she was able to connect cause and consequence:

> But now she knows it all being dead.
> Great people lived and died in this house
> ...
> But he killed the house; to kill a house
> Where great men grew-up, married, died,
> I here declare a capital offence.[100]

It is the Old Man who speaks these lines, her son who sees the havoc wrought by passion. Thus Yeats presented in dramatic terms the idea that the relationship between cause and consequence is inviolable. Not only does passion create destiny, it also causes a temporary obscuring of reason, as noted earlier. Thus acted Diarmuid in *The Dreaming of the Bones*, and the woman in *Purgatory*.

Yeats's play *The Words Upon the Window-Pane* presents in dramatic terms the contrast between *Passionate Body* and *Spirit*; the former is represented by Vanessa and the latter by Stella.[101] Vanessa's love for Swift is all passion and no thought:

> I thought it would be enough to look at you, to speak to you, to hear you speak. I followed you to Ireland five years ago and I can bear it no longer. ...Jonathan, Jonathan, I am a woman, the women Brutus and Cato loved were not different.

Stella's words on the other hand are reason itself:

> You taught how I might youth prolong
> By knowing what is right and wrong;
> How from my heart to bring supplies
> Of lustre to my fading eyes...

Fate or necessity is that which is brought about by following the dictates of discriminative mind, *buddhi* or reason, not of passion. Reason prompts a detached view of the situation, based upon knowledge of right and wrong, whereas passion is narrow and selfish. Both Swift and Stella have outgrown *Passionate Body* and are guided by *Spirit*. Yeats examines Swift's motives for celibacy in *The Words Upon the Window-Pane*, and presents the idea that his decision was guided by personal considerations as well as by his view of the historical situation. The ghost of Swift says: "I have something in my blood that no child must inherit. I have constant attacks of dizziness...."[102] The real reason may be that his passionate nature is not entirely worn out yet, and at times borders on the insane; the ghost of Vanessa refers to him as the most passionate man in Ireland. Swift has realized that an act and its consequences affect not only the doer but also spread out in expanding ripples to affect the whole state. As another character in the play, John Corbet says, Swift's ideal political order was the Roman Senate, and he foresaw its reversal in the coming of democracy, and so dreaded the future. Vanessa says her blood is healthy and will make their children healthy, but Swift associated the word "healthy" with the body and its passions, with the common mind and democracy. "Am I to add another to the healthy rascaldom and knavery of the world?"[103] "He hated the common run of men," says John Corbet. What distinguishes great men is their intellect that makes them tower above the crowd; Swift's ideal men were Brutus and Cato. Swift's own reason prevails when he prays to God that he may bequeath to posterity "his intellect that came to him from Heaven."[104] The same contrast between *Passionate Body* and *Celestial Body* is presented in the characters of Congal and Attracta. Attracta who is intellect or *buddhi* says: "I burn/ Not in the flesh but in the mind...."[105]

The concept of rebirth in the Upaniṣads involves a process that brings about spiritual growth. Man lives through phases of bodily, emotional, intellectual, and spiritual growth during a period spread over many lifetimes. Yeats renders the same idea through specific symbolism when he says that in the wheel of the *Principles*, *Husk* predominates during the first quarter, *Passionate Body* during the second, *Spirit* during the third, and *Celestial Body* during the fourth.[106] He explains the same thing more clearly in his introduction to *The Holy Mountain*: "we must exhaust ambition, intellect, desire, dedicating all things as they pass, or we come to God with empty hands."[107] Yeats wrote 'The Four Ages of Man', defining the four stages in man's development, as based on the *Four Principles*.[108] The underlying idea is that the soul must find fulfillment in every way, gather all kinds of experience, before it seeks renunciation and merges in the Absolute. For instance, when one outgrows *Passionate Body* and evolves towards *Celestial Body*, one leaves behind certain relationships, and forms new ones that are in greater harmony with one's changed personality. This idea is presented by Yeats in *The Only Jealousy of Emer,* where Cuchulain's Daimon or guiding spirit, personified as the Figure of Cuchulain, bids Emer renounce the love of Cuchulain as he has found a new attraction in Ethne Inguba. If Emer does not renounce Cuchulain, the bond will persist in a future life. The Daimon explains to her that in future she will not be his wife; there will be "a strange woman/ Besides his mattress." The Daimon asks Emer:

> You've watched his loves and have not been jealous,
> Knowing that he would tire, but do those tire
> That love the Sidhe?[109]

Cuchulain in his many loves is really seeking his own ultimate self represented by Woman of the Sidhe in the play. She is a representation of the enlightened personality symbolized by the full moon, "Shedding such light from limb and hair/ As when the moon,…/ Flings out upon the fifteenth night."[110] Similarly, in *The Words Upon the Window Pane*, Swift has outgrown *Passionate Body,* and has moved to *Celestial Body*; correspondingly, his relationship with Vanessa comes to an end, and a new relationship is formed with Stella.

Mohini Chatterjee had taught the Theosophists, that the soul lives through many incarnations. In a paper he read to the London Lodge of the Theosophical Society he had said:

> This life is only one out of the numberless patterns which the ceaseless motion of the kaleidoscope of existence produces.[111]

As noted earlier, Yeats recorded in his *Memoirs* that he had been sceptical of this doctrine, at that time.[112] In 1928, he wrote the poem 'Mohini Chatterjee' expressing his gratitude to the person who had first spoken to him about the immortality of the soul through many births; Chatterjee had asked him to sing that he had been a king, a slave, "Fool rascal, knave…." Yeats added "in commentary" the knowledge gained from his study of the Upaniṣads that many incarnations were given to man so that he found fulfillment. Yeats accepted this philosophy joyously, as to him it meant fulfillment of love relationships:

> Old lovers yet may have
> All that time denied —
> Grave is heaped on grave
> That they be satisfied— [113]

Time seems to deny this fulfillment as death interrupts relationships; however, burial is not something final; he affirmed later in 'Under Ben Bulben':

> Whether man die in his bed
> Or the rifle knocks him dead,
> A brief parting from those dear
> Is the worst man has to fear.[114]

The doctrine of rebirth in the Upaniṣads offered him consolation. Those who were buried, lived "in the human mind," and would meet again in a future incarnation.

Of the two alternatives offered in the Upaniṣads, ascetic life versus active, enlightened life, Yeats chose the latter, as the former implied escaping from "the crime of birth and death." To escape rebirth would be to attain the void of eternity, "the wintry blast" of 'A Dialogue of Self and Soul.' Death was irrelevant as the soul was immortal: "Men dance on deathless feet."

There comes a stage, however, when every crime is expiated, every relationship exhausted, and every experience fulfilled. This is the state of dreamless sleep[115] when the soul must, as it were, "close its eyes." There is yet a further condition, a fourth state: "This fourth stage, pure light to those that reach it, is that state wherein the soul, as much ancient symbolism testifies, is united to the blessed dead."[116] The two stages, whether experienced in life or in death, are in the Upaniṣads considered states of final enlightenment, and correspond to Yeats's concept of Unity of Being.

Yeats wrote that his accounts of after-death states, particularly of the *Dreaming Back*, differed from those of Swedenborg because the latter did not consider rebirth.[117] In the Upaniṣads on the other hand, although he found no detailed accounts of the states between death and rebirth, everywhere he found belief in immortality. The *Bhagavad*

Gītā expresses it thus:

> Weapons do not cleave this self,
> Fire does not burn him.[118]

It is this idea that Yeats portrays dramatically through the futile attempt of Congal to kill the Herne with stones, or to cut him up with swords. Congal finally realizes that the Herne

> is god and out of reach;
> Nor stone can bruise, nor a sword pierce him....[119]

The Upaniṣads present the idea that identification of the Self with the body or any other object is ignorance, and brings despair. In the *Chāndogya Upaniṣad*, Wirochana among the demons, and Indra among the godly, go to Prajapati for instruction on the immortal Self. Wirochana identifies the Self with the physical body. Indra, however, has his doubts regarding this philosophy:

> If the body is adorned, so is its reflection...but then if the body were blind, Self would be blind...if the body were dead, Self would be dead, I see no good in this.

Prajapati finally teaches him that the body is mortal, yet it houses the immortal spirit.[120] In 'Among School Children' Yeats presents the idea that identification of the Self with the body can only bring despair. If the mother of the newborn child thinks of its appearance as it will be in future, the "shape/ With sixty or more winters on its head," she will find no compensation for her pangs. Only faith in the immortality of the soul brings joy.

Yeats found that the experience of the tragic hero and that of the sage coincide. Neither identifies himself with the body, hence its ageing or passing away causes no pang; rather, their knowledge of immortality transforms despair into joy: the soldier becomes the sage when in some Elizabethan tragedy he shrugs off a threat of hanging with: "What has that to do with me?"[121] Yeats goes on to say that Mohini Chatterjee taught philosophy to a man who denied the soul's immortality with the same words. Yeats found this affirmation of the soul's supremacy in all Shakespeare's last words and closing scenes, in speeches like Hamlet's exhortation to Horatio to hold off felicity; in 'Lapis Lazuli' he said:

> ...Hamlet and Lear are gay;
> Gaiety transfiguring all that dread.[122]

Through his visits to séances, through experiment and experience, Yeats sought to confirm the truths of the Upaniṣads. The occult tradition of experiment that existed in ancient India, before these truths were finally formulated in the Upaniṣads, is now lost. It must be acknowledged that Yeats sought to restore a similar Western tradition providing data towards proof of immortality. He was aware that he was swimming against the stream of prevailing scepticism on this score in the modern age. This is evidenced in an impassioned note to Olivia Shakespear, in which he spoke of his dream of "a wild paper for the young," which would be suppressed, possibly a number of times, "for the logical assertion, with all fitting deductions, of the immortality of the soul."[123] As we have seen above, many of his poems and plays were written to amplify these "deductions" from the premise of immortality.

Notes

1 *Vision* (B), p.220.

2 *Bṛhad-āraṇyaka Upaniṣad*, IV, 2.1.

3 *Chāndogya Upaniṣad*, V.3.2.

4 *Kaṭha Upaniṣad*, I.1.29–II .2.8.

5 See *Autobiographies*, p.15.

6 *Essays*, p.513.

7 A.O. Hume, *Hints on Esoteric Theosophy* (Calcutta: The Calcutta Central Press Co. Ltd., 1882), p.38.

8 A.P. Sinnett, *Esoteric Buddhism* (London: The Theosophical Publishing House Ltd., 1972); see chapters on "Devachan" and "Kama Loka."

9 See *Memoirs*, p.24. Yeats seems to have somewhat anticipated this reaction, as he recorded on 20 December 1889: "I proposed scheme for organization of occult research. Matter referred to H.P.B. H.P.B. will refuse probably on the ground of danger by opening up means of black magic." *Ibid.*, p.282.

10 See *Esoteric Buddhism*, p.91: "The more frequently it is appealed to by the affection of friends...the more vehement will be the impulses which draw it back to physical life, and the more serious the retardation of its spiritual progress. This consideration appears to involve the most influential motive which leads the representatives of theosophical teaching to discountenance and disapprove of all attempts to hold communication with departed souls by means of the spiritual séance."

11 See *Autobiographies*, p.149.

12 W.B. Yeats, *Fairy and Folk Tales of the Irish Peasantry* (London: Walter Scott, 1888), p.ix. Hence cited as *Fairy and Folk Tales.*

13 *Stories from Carleton* (London: The Camelot Series, 1889); *Irish Fairy Tales* (London: Fisher Unwin, 1892); *The Celtic Twilight* (London: Lawrence and Bullen, 1893).

14 *Fairy and Folk Tales*, p.xv.

15 See *Mythologies*, p.63.

16 Augusta Gregory, *Visions and Beliefs in the West of Ireland* (New York and London: The Knickerbocker Press, 1920). Hence cited as *Visions and Beliefs*.

17 *Memoirs*, p.49.

18 *Ibid*., p.48.

19 (a) *Ibid*., pp.47–49.

(b) See John Kelly and Eric Domville, ed. *The Collected Letters of W.B. Yeats: Vol.I 1865-–1895* (Oxford: Clarendon Press, 1986), p.267. The editors explain (in a footnote to Yeats's letter to George Russell) as to how the apparition was evoked using the Golden Dawn symbols. Hence cited as *Collected Letters of Yeats*.

20 *Memoirs*, p.49.

21 Unpublished letter.

22 See *Essays*, p.517.

23 *Visions and Beliefs*, see Yeats's notes, pp.278–79.

24 See *Explorations* (London: Macmillan and Co. Ltd., 1962), p.51. In 'Swedenborg, Mediums, and the Desolate Places' Yeats mentions the following writers: Aksakof, Myers, Lodge, Flammarion, Flournoy, Maxwell, Albert de Rochas, Lombroso, Ochorowicz and Hyslop.

25 See *Transactions of the London Lodge*, No.1.

26 See *Transactions of the London Lodge*, No.3.

27 *Īśa Upaniṣad*, I.

28 *From the Upanishads*, p.ix.

29 See Charles Johnston, *The Memory of Past Births* (New York: The Metaphysical Publishing Co., 1899), p.5.

30 *Works and Wisdom*, p.19.

31 (a) *Vision* (A), p.354.

(b) The work Florence Farr referred to was *Yoga Vashistha Maharamayana* of Valmiki. Also see *Letters to Yeats*, p.254.

32 *Memoirs*, "Journal" entry July 1913, p.266.

33 *Essays*, p.517.

34 *Vision* (B), p.220.

35 *Bṛhad-āraṇyaka Upaniṣad*, IV.3.11; also see Śaṁkara's comment on this verse.

36 See *Vision* (B), p.221.

37 See *Vision* (B), p.222.

38 *Mythologies*, p.356.

39 *Ibid.*, p.363.

40 See *Essays*, p.469.

41 *Bṛhad-āraṇyaka Upaniṣad*, VI.2.15.

42 *Ibid.*, VI.2.16.

43 *Praśna Upaniṣad*, 1.4.

44 See *Kaṭha Upaniṣad*, II.2.9; also see *Praśna Upaniṣad*, I.5.

45 Commenting on *Kaṭha*, I.3.13, Radhakrishnan explains: "The wise disciple should discriminate the unchanging light, the *ātman*, from the changing objects of sense and mind which it illumines, *an-ātman*." *The Principle Upaniṣads*, p.628. See also *Secret Doctrine*, pp.86–87.

46 *Vision* (B), p.219.

47 *Ibid.*, p.190.

48 *Ibid.*

49 See *Transactions of the London Lodge*, No.3, p.7.

50 *Mythologies*, p.104.

51 See *Vision* (B), p.16.

[52] See *Vision* (A), p.160.

[53] See *Vision* (B), p.193.

[54] *Ibid.*, p.188.

[55] *Ibid.*, p.158.

[56] *Ibid.*, p.189.

[57] *Bṛhad-āraṇyaka Upaniṣad*, IV.3.38.

[58] *Ibid.*, IV.4.2.

[59] *Concept of Ātman*, p.146.

[60] Hume, *Bṛhad-āraṇyaka Upaniṣad*, III.2.13.

[61] See *Vision* (B), p.189.

[62] *Vision* (B), p.222.

[63] *Praśna* Upaniṣad, III, 10.

[64] Hume, *Chāndogya Upaniṣad*, VIII.2.10.

[65] *Esoteric Buddhism,* p.62.

[66] See *Bṛhad-āraṇyaka Upaniṣad*, III.3.1.

[67] *Ibid.*, IV.3.11.

[68] *Ibid.*, IV.4.6.

[69] *Purgatory, Collected Plays*, p.682.

[70] *Explorations*, p.331.

[71] *Ibid.*

[72] See *The Death of Cuchulain, Collected Plays*, p.703.

[73] *Purgatory, Collected Plays*, pp.685, 688.

[74] (a) *Vision* (B), p.226.

(b) See also *Explorations*, p.366: "They examine their past if undisturbed by our importunity, tracing events to their source, and as they take the form their thought suggests, seem to live backward through time..."

[75] *Collected Poems*, p.267.

[76] *Ibid.*, p.185.

[77] *Ibid.*, p.281.

[78] See *Mythologies*, p.21.

[79] See *Taittirīya Upaniṣad*, II.6.1.

[80] See *Vision* (B), p.224.

[81] *Īśa Upaniṣad*, 3.

[82] *Transactions of the London Lodge*, No.1, pp.3, 18.

[83] *Collected Plays*, p.440.

[84] See *Bṛhad-āraṇyaka* Upaniṣad, IV.3.20.

[85] See *Kaṭha Upaniṣad*, II.2.6.

[86] *Vision* (B), p.238.

[87] *Collected Plays*, p.647.

[88] (a) Sinnett had explained that the after-death state was not a life of responsibility: "It is a life of *effects*, not of *causes*." *Esoteric Buddhism*, p.63.

(b) Yeats acknowledged of the *Dreaming Back* that "there can be nothing new..." *Vision* (B), p.226.

[89] Hume, *Chāndogya Upaniṣad*, VIII.1.6.

[90] See *Bṛhad-āraṇyaka Upaniṣad*, IV.4.6.

[91] See *Vision* (B), p.190.

[92] *Indian Philosophy*, I, 211.

[93] *Vision* (B), p.219.

[94] See Hume, *Kaṭha Upaniṣad*, II.1. This and the next five verses are marked in Yeats's copy, p.346.

[95] See *Vision* (B), p.239.

[96] *Explorations*, p.344.

97 *Collected Plays*, p.442.

98 *Ibid.*, p.443.

99 *Ibid.*, p.682.

100 *Ibid.*, p.683.

101 *Ibid.*, pp.609, 613.

102 (a) *Ibid.*, p.609.

(b) Yeats wrote in his introduction to *The Words Upon The Window Pane* that Swift's dread of madness was the theme of his play. See *Explorations*, p.360.

103 *Ibid.*, p.610.

104 *Ibid.*, p.611.

105 *Ibid.*, p.650.

106 See *Vision* (B), p.192.

107 *Essays* p.483.

108 See *Collected Poems*, p.332.

109 *Collected Plays*, p.289.

110 *Ibid.*, p.291.

111 *Transactions of the London Lodge*, No.3, p.10. (Paper read on 10 December, 1884.)

112 See *Memoirs*, p.48.

113 *Collected Poems*, p.279.

114 *Ibid.*, p.398.

115 See *Vision* (B), p.220. Dreamless sleep is one of the states of the soul in the Upaniṣads.

116 *Vision* (B), p.222.

117 See *Vision* (B), p.227, Yeats's footnote no. 3.

118 *The Bhagavad-Gīta*, II.23.

119 *Collected Plays*, p.662.

120 See Yeats and Swāmi, pp.113–15.

121 *Explorations*, p.296.

122 (a) *Collected Poems*, p.338.

(b) Lady Gregory, who shared this view, rejected many a play "in the modern manner" sent to the Abbey Theatre, saying: "Tragedy must be a joy to the man who dies." See *Essays*, p.523.

123 *Letters*, p.706.

Chapter Four

"Unity of Being"

> When Pearse summoned Cuchulain to his side,
> What stalked through the Post Office? What intellect,
> What calculation, number, measurement, replied?
>
> — 'The Statues'

Searching for ancient sources for the phases of the moon as revealed to him by his instructors, Yeats found a striking parallel between his own symbolism and the references in the Upaniṣads to the bright and dark fortnights. He found the symbolism unique to the Upaniṣads and Indian philosophy, yet there were similarities with his own work:

> I do not remember the brightening and darkening fortnights in any classical author, but they are in the Upanishads and in the Laws of Manu...[1]

Yeats went on to say that the basic symbolism with its opposition between light and dark "concerned him most." In his introduction to *The Holy Mountain*, Yeats summed up the distinction between the two paths leading to unity of being, symbolized by the bright and dark fortnights as explained in the Upaniṣads. "Here and there in the *Upanishads* mention is made of the moon's bright fortnight, the nights from the new to the full moon, and of the dark fortnight of the moon decline." The way of the bright fortnight and the full moon, was the way of wisdom or the Gods "expressed or symbolized in the senses." On the other hand, the way of the dark fortnight and the dark moon, was one of piety and of peace in the interim between death and rebirth. "The *Upanishads* denied any escape for these."[2]

Various Upaniṣads discuss the relative merits of these paths: among them are the *Bṛhad-āraṇyaka*, the *Chāndogya,* the *Praśna* and the *Muṇḍaka* Upaniṣads. The *Bṛhad-āraṇyaka Upaniṣad,* for instance, says that those who belong to the bright fortnight meditate on the truth. "In those worlds of Brahma they live for long periods. Of these there is no return." Against this, those who live in the dark fortnight, perform sacrifices and practice charity and austerity, go to the world of the fathers and thence to the moon. Finally, they are reborn on the earth. "Thus do they rotate."[3] The central symbol here is the moon, which is a classic symbol of the mind of man.[4] As the sage Yājñavalkya explains, the fortnights are symbolic of two contrasting ways of spiritual life, each culminating in a different experience of unity. Yeats learnt from the Upaniṣads that the bright fortnight culminated in the full moon symbolic of enlightened consciousness, a waking state, termed by the Upaniṣads *Turīya*: "the bright fortnight's escape is *Turīya.*" The dark fortnight culminated in the dark moon signifying unconscious merger in God referred to as *Suṣupti* or dreamless sleep.

Both these states represent unity of the individual with his deepest self. The former is antithetical and subjective, termed "Unity of Being" by Yeats, while the latter is a primary and objective unity. Yeats's own symbols of the dark moon and the full moon, or phases one and fifteen respectively symbolize these states. Yeats imagined *Turīya* as symbolised by the full moon, mirror-like bright water, and Mount Meru; *Suṣupti* by moonl ess night, "dazzling darkness" and Mount Girnar. Yeats discovered a similar symbolism in Western thought:

> A European would think perhaps of the moonlit and moonless nights alone, call the increasing moon man's personality, as it fills into the round and becomes perfect, overthrowing the black night of oblivion.[5]

In Yeats, as also in the Upaniṣads, the sun symbolizes ultimate truth and the moon the individual. In *A Vision*, from phase one to phase fifteen, the moon or the individual slowly increases in light. At the fifteenth phase, the moon possesses full light from the sun; the individual possesses his personality as subject and knowledge of the ultimate as the underlying unity. Yeats realized that his symbol of the full moon representing apotheosis of personality corresponded closely to the state *Turīya* described in the Upaniṣads.

He narrates in his introduction to *The Holy Mountain* that the mystic symbol *aum* symbolizing the state *Turīya* was sung by a liberated soul, and heard by Bhagwān Shri Hamsa upon Mount Kailāśa. The symbol *aum* signifies the *Ātman* or the Self present in all beings as well as states of consciousness, though only the liberated soul is aware of it, as he identifies himself with it. Yeats analyses the significance of *aum*, which stands for the four states of consciousness, in his introductions to *The Holy Mountain* and *The Māṇḍūkya Upaniṣad.* These are: "the waking state corresponding to the letter 'A', where physical objects are present; the dream state corresponding to the letter 'U', where mental objects are present; the state of dreamless sleep corresponding to the letter 'M', where all seems darkness to the soul, because all there is lost in Brahma, creator of mental and physical objects; the final state corresponding to the whole sacred word '*AUM*'*;* consciousness bound to no object, bliss bound to no aim, *Turīya*, pure personality."[6]

The state of *Turīya* in the Upaniṣads is a complete consciousness of unity where there is identification between subject and object: in Yeats's words, "a moon that has taken the sun's light." *Turīya* is "the fourth" and indicates the final stage in meditation. According to the *Māṇḍūkya Upaniṣad:*

> The fourth is that which has no elements, which cannot be spoken of, into which the world is resolved, benign, non-dual. Thus the syllable *aum* is the very self. He who knows it thus enters the self with his self.[7]

Radhakrishnan explains in his commentary on this verse in *The Principal Upaniṣads*, that here there is "neither the perception nor the idea of God…It is reality, spirit in its inner life." In Yeats's words "full *Turīya* or 'seedless' *Samādhi* comes when all these states are as a single timeless act, and that act is pure or unimpeded personality, all existence brought into the words: 'I am.'"[8] "Pure personality" is Yeats's term for *Turīya*, which is really a state of realization on the part of the aspirant that he is none else, but the Absolute or *Brahman.*[9]

That Yeats had studied this idea of the self as unity is very clear from the passages marked in his copy of *The Thirteen Principal Upanishads* translated by R.E. Hume. In the chapter entitled, 'Idealism and the Conception of Pure Unity' he had underlined the following definitions:

> The final unity could not and would not, then, be found outside of self, but in it. In truth, the self is the unity they had been looking for all along…[10]

and

> that world-ground, that unity of being...is none other than the self...

Yeats too spoke of his own faith in Unity of Being; it was what Dante had compared to a perfectly proportioned human body and the Upaniṣads had called "Self."[11]

Yeats saw that it was possible to understand the full moon as symbolic of a final maturing into this state of realization, perfection of personality. Yeats's early knowledge of this truth was intuitive, but was augmented by the revelations of *A Vision*, and finally perfected by his reading of the Upaniṣads and discussions with Shree Purohit Swāmi. In 1909 he was still groping for this unity when he wrote the following:

> The soul knows its changes of state alone, and I think the motives of tragedy are not related to action but to changes of state. I feel this but do not see clearly, for I am hunting truth into its thicket...[12]

In 1910, he wrote with greater confidence that of all forms of art, tragic art was the one form that evoked the unity experienced by mystics in their moments of trance.[13]

As discussed in the chapter on Nature, Yeats accepted the view of the Upaniṣads that ultimate reality falls in human consciousness into a series of antinomies. These antinomies are the *Four Principles: Husk, Passionate Body, Spirit, and Celestial Body*, which appear to be divided into subject and object, the microcosm and the macrocosm. Unity is achieved through a process of realizing that the *Principles* are fragments of a whole that may be symbolized by the sphere.

The *Kaṭha Upaniṣad* explains that when the senses cease to be preoccupied with the external world, and the mind turns inward to a contemplation of its own essential form, the Divine or the Self is revealed.[14] Yeats refers to this opening of the inner eye, as it were, as "the opening of the tinctures." Yeats explains: "The opening means the reflection inward of the *Four Faculties*: all are as it were mirrored in personality, Unity of Being becomes possible. Hitherto we have been part of something else, but now discover everything within our own nature."[15] Yeats's poems 'Sailing to Byzantium' and 'Byzantium' create a picture of this state of mind, the culmination of the process in which the mind turns away from the objects of senses and passions. The state pictured in "the young in one another's arms," gives way to one wherein "the unpurged images of day recede." The city of the body has become the city of Byzantium; the Emperor or the spirit is all-powerful. It is stated in the Upaniṣads that in sleep, meditation and liberation, "He breaks the link with all that belongs to the body; he remains awake giving light…He is the Golden God, the Man, the Self, Hamsa, the solitary Bird."[16] It is a vision of this self, "an image, man or shade,/ Shade more than man, more image than a shade," that Yeats sees in the depths of contemplation. This experience he called 'Byzantium', because he felt that in Western history the Christian civilization of Byzantium came closest to mirroring it. "I think that in early Byzantium, may be never before or since in recorded history, religious, aesthetic and practical life were one..."[17] Byzantium represents not only unity of culture but also unity of being: the seer having gained pure consciousness in the mystical state of *Turīya*, experiences the one life pervading the physical, emotional, mental, and spiritual consciousness. Purohit Swāmi comments that through a process of meditation the *yogi* finally arrives at a stage when he says, "I am Spirit, the personal Self is the impersonal Self," a state in which he remains forever. "All these four conditions of illumination lead to unmixed conscious illumination which is final."[18] In the *Bṛhad-āraṇyaka Upaniṣad,* Yājñavalkya explains that the man who is free from desires is one whose desire is the self; such a man becomes *Brahman.*[19]

Renunciation of desire is freedom; liberation does not signify escape of the soul from the body, but a fusion of the two in a life lived for higher purposes, for things "vaster than the individual," in Yeats's phrase. To be liberated while living is man's highest goal. Such beings, purified of personal desire, are described in 'Byzantium' as "blood-begotten spirits." Yeats refers to their state of blessedness as "death-in-life and life-in-death," in a phrase which is really an adequate rendering of the Sanskrit term *jīvan-mukta*, or one who is liberated during his lifetime. The faculties are merely instrumental in arriving at this unity. Bhagwān Shri Hamsa explained it thus:

> …the Ahankar along with Buddhi, Chitta, Antahkaran and Manas—all merged into the Absolute Brahma! I found myself reflected everywhere in the whole Universe! It was all one harmony—full of Wisdom, Infinite Love Perennial and Bliss Eternal! Where was the body, its tenements and the 'I'! It was all Satchidānanda (Truth, Wisdom and Bliss).[20]

This is *Turīya*, literally "the fourth stage" termed by Yeats "pure personality":

> In pure personality, seedless *Samādhi*, there is nothing but that bare 'I am' which is Brahma. The initiate, all old Karma exhausted, is 'the Human Form Divine' of Blake, that Unity of Being Dante compared to a perfectly proportioned human body...[21]

Another aspect of the enlightened soul is great physical beauty which is essentially a form assumed by the immanent self, the self present in senses, body, mind and intellect alike, and illumining them all. Yeats's symbol for this spiritual perfection is superhuman physical beauty in life, "marmorean stillness," and the perfection of a statue in art. The *Bṛhad-āraṇyka Upaniṣad* clearly states that when the soul, working through many births attains enlightenment, it takes on a beautiful body, just as a goldsmith fashions a new and beautiful shape from a piece of gold.[22]

The fifteenth phase in Yeats is a phase of "complete beauty," wherein the person possesses the body which the soul will permanently inhabit, when all phases destined for it have been lived out.[23] Yeats numbers among those nearly perfect beings Helen (at phase fourteen). This beauty is the result of self-realization accompanying long suffering. As he puts it in his poem, 'The Phases of the Moon,' it is the result of "some bloody whip in their own hands," and "the strange reward of all that discipline." In 'Under Ben Bulben' Yeats exhorts poets and countrymen to "Swear...by those women/ Complexion and form prove superhuman..."

Unity of Being as beauty or a well-proportioned body is the complete fusion of senses, body, mind, and spirit in the personality of man. The *Kaṭha Upaniṣad* refers to the integrated personality in 'The Parable of the Chariot,' wherein the Self is the lord of the chariot, which is the body, and the intellect and the mind are the charioteer and the reins respectively.[24] The self-enlightened intellect controls the reins of the mind, which in turn controls the senses. The Upaniṣad advocates not rejection but control of the senses; the senses and the mind have each their proportionate importance and are not be rejected altogether, but used as instruments of the spirit.

This very idea is the theme of Yeats's poem, 'Among School Children.' He presents the integrated personality of the dancer exemplifying the fusion of body, mind and spirit, and opposes it to other kinds of existence in which the body, mind or intellect are given disproportionate importance. The latter kind of existence is never able to encompass the whole truth. Reality is not merely an intellectual construct, a formula, but rapport of the whole being of man with the entire universe. The word used in the Upaniṣads to indicate supreme reality is *brahman*. It is derived from the root *brh*, which means to grow or to burst forth. Thus the real is not an abstraction; it is the dynamic movement between the essence and its manifestation, the true life of the whole. It is this view that Yeats renders poetically in 'Among School Children':

> O Chestnut tree, great rooted blossomer,
> Are you the leaf, the blossom or the bole?
> O body swayed to music, O brightening glance,
> How can we know the dancer from the dance?

Explaining this in greater detail in his essay, 'The Mandukya Upanishad,' Yeats says: "we must not think of it as a target, as something struck or seized when subject or object unite, but as the sole being that is completely alive, completely active; our approach is revelation."[25] To know the self is to become it, hence in the highest spiritual experience the idea of adoration of a separate God becomes redundant. In the Upaniṣads Vāmadeva declares: "Whoever worships another divinity (than his self) thinking that he is one and (*Brahman*) another, he knows not."[26] In 'Among School Children' Yeats declares in a similar vein,

> Both nuns and mothers worship images...
> And yet they too break hearts—

and rejects worship that implies a separation between subject and object.

In *Turīya*, the sage, seer or poet, knowing all, has become the self of all. In this state the sage or seer is free to act, to sing of truths, or to remain absorbed in silence. *Aum* or the sacred chant symbolic of this state represents the three divisions of time into past, present and future, the three states of consciousness, as well as the state that transcends the threefold division of time.[27] Yeats too says in 'Sailing to Byzantium' that he wishes to arrive at this state and sing of "what is past, or passing, or to come."

Opposed to the conscious, illumined personality of the fifteenth phase, is the complete submission of the self to God at phase one: in the primary phases "unity is moral." Yeats sees *Suṣupti* or dreamless sleep as symbolized by "moonless night, 'dazzling darkness.'"[28] He first made an effort to understand *Suṣupti* or dreamless sleep while working on his introduction to *The Holy Mountain*. He wrote to Purohit Swāmi: "The point is important to me. I am deep in your master's travels that is why I care to know."[29] In a letter written sometime later, he indicated that he had consulted the works of E. Roer as well as Sir Arthur Keith on *Suṣupti*.[30] *Suṣupti* is the third of the four states of the soul, while *Turīya*, discussed above, is the fourth. The state of *Suṣupti* or deep sleep is explained in the *Māṇḍukya Upaniṣad* as *prājña*, or the state where one becomes "a mass of cognition," and is full of bliss. Here there is no desire or dream whatsoever.[31] It is described by Radhakrishnan as "the conceptual self" or inactive consciousness. Yeats underlined the following sentence in his copy of Radhakrishnan's *Indian Philosophy*: "Śaṁkara observes that the phenomena of duality caused by the action of the mind are present in the other two conditions, but absent here. In several passages we are told that we taste the nature of absolute bliss in dreamless sleep, where a man is cut off from the distracting world."[32] Yeats explained the same idea in his essay on 'The Mandukya Upanishad,' saying that dreamless sleep is called "conscious" because one is "united to sleepless Self, creator of all, source of all." This is a state which cannot be known, only experienced as union with that Self.[33]

Although the state is indescribable, ungraspable, Patanjali examines the different stages or steps of *samādhi* or concentration that lead to it. Both Purohit Swāmi and Yeats have commented on these stages. The former explains how an object for meditation is consciously chosen in the waking state, but as trance deepens, thinker and object become one. According to him, "the thinker, the thinking, the thought are one; the meditations have reached their climax and are still; the sculptor, the marble block, are gone, but the statue remains."[34] Echoing Purohit Swāmi's words, Yeats defines *Suṣupti* as the third stage in meditation wherein "the man has disappeared as the sculptor in his statue, the musician in his music."[35]

In Yeats's symbolism, phase one corresponds to the attainment of this unity or *Suṣupti*, and the last three phases of the moon to stages of concentration that lead to it through austerity. As phase one entirely symbolizes *Suṣupti*, it must be regarded as the parent metaphor and examined first:

> Phase 1 is called Moon in Sun because the lunar or *antithetical tincture* is consumed in the *primary* or solar, but from another point of view it is the *Body of Fate* consumed in *Creative Mind*; man is submissive and plastic...[36]

The first part of the statement refers to complete merger, a state where in the absence of the subjective knower, objective knowledge cannot be defined, but may be experienced. In the second part, use of the word "submissive" indicates a conscious surrender to a transcendent power. Yeats explains this merger of the subjective into the objective by saying that thought and inclination, desire and its object are one. In other words, individual ego or conditioned consciousness (regarded in the Upaniṣads as the result of *avidyā* or nescience) is annihilated by the dawn of knowledge that the individual soul is really the Supreme Spirit. The mind and its objects of knowledge are merged into each other, become one mass of cognition referred to in the Upaniṣads as *prajñānaghana*. Desire has vanished in the total acceptance of fact. Whereas in *Turīya* or "pure personality," there may be control over the senses and desires, and objects of the world enjoyed with detachment, in *Suṣupti* there is complete cessation of desire and suppression of the senses. Patanjali refers to this complete obliteration of personality as *asamprajñāta samādhi.* Purohit Swāmi renders it thus:

> Asampradnyāta Samādhi is that unmixed condition of conscious illumination, where by constant renunciation of all knowledge, mind retains past impressions only.[37]

He explains that in this state the *yogi* does not desire even spiritual knowledge and its power; his mind goes beyond love and hate and accepts its fate as the result of past ḳarma. He renounces all desire, because of which the last impressions on the mind are obliterated and the mind merges in Self. In Yeats's terminology, *Mask* is discarded in acceptance of *Body of Fate*, and desire or *Will* disappears in *Creative Mind.*[38] The Upaniṣads refer to such a person as *videhamukta*, one liberated completely from the body; in Yeats's phase one, "body is completely absorbed in its supernatural environment."

Beings of the last primary phases conform to the definition of the dark fortnight. It is instructive to trace this surrender of the self or personality as it appears in phases twenty-six, twenty-seven, and twenty-eight, referred to as phases of the hunchback, the saint, and the fool, in *A Vision*. Opposed to great personal beauty of beings near the full moon, here there is great deformity symbolized by the hunchback, and is the result of lack of desire or mask, the power that shapes from within:

> Deformed, because there is no deformity
> But saves us from a dream.[39]

Only God now out of reach, possesses perfection; Yeats says of these:

> ...having no desire they cannot tell
> What's good or bad, or what it is to triumph
> At the perfection of one' own obedience...

Instead, there is submission to a code imposed from without: the saint attains *Suṣupti* through subduing his physical senses and meditating upon a divine personality. At phase twenty-eight we have the fool, who is close to the state that is indefinable and ungraspable, he himself as non-descript as it is possible for a human type to be. He has "no active intelligence" exemplifying the inactive consciousness of *Suṣupti.* As the symbol of this state is the darkening moon, the thoughts as well as acts of the fool are "aimless," yet as the phase is also nearest the sun or objective knowledge, "he would know all wisdom if he could know anything."[40] Yeats describes the desireless man of the twenty-eighth phase as "a straw blown by the wind," who drifts about, and is sometimes referred to as "The Child of God." Senses, mind, and intellect form individual consciousness, which reflects the all-pervasive consciousness. In deep sleep, "the reflecting medium, having gone fully dormant, there is no more any capable medium which may reflect the all-pervasive consciousness in any form. In the absence of any reflecting medium, the individual consciousness (jīva) merges into the all-pervasive conscious-ness."[41]

Yeats considered the relative merits of these two ideals of unity presented in the Upaniṣads as *Turīya* and *Suṣupti* or as *jivanmukti* and *videhamukti*; he referred to them as unity of man and unity of God,[42] or as the antithetical and primary aspects of unity. In 'The

Double Vision of Michael Robartes' he admitted

> Being caught between the pull
> Of the dark moon and the full...

Although the ideal symbolized by the dark moon is upheld in the scriptures as the *summum bonum* of life, yet it is neither recommended by Indian philosophic tradition,[43] nor subscribed to by Yeats. Yeats defined Unity of Being as "a reality which is concrete, sensuous, bodily." The poems, 'A Dialogue of Self and Soul' and 'Vacillation' carry on this weighing of opposite ideals.

Yeats examined all history, East and West, in terms of these two ideals. The cycle of the seasons patterned upon the dark and bright fortnights could provide the symbolical framework wherein he could examine the history of the world.[44] It became possible to see that every civilization discovered alternately the subjective and objective aspects of its particular religion. Yeats found that the thinkers of the Upaniṣads represented a unity consciously understood, and replaced an earlier culture. Yājñavalkaya and his school replaced an earlier popular religion, "the trance of the soma drinkers...or that induced by beaten drums...."[45] These sages discovered *Turīya,* where the soul attains purity and its own state of timelessness.

Like Hinduism, Christianity too is alternately primary and antithetical. In the beginning God is seen as above and beyond man, but "night will fall upon man's wisdom now that man has been taught that he is nothing."[46] This primary phase gives way to the antithetical when the Byzantine civilization flowers at the fifteenth phase of its moon. It is a likeness of the Sacred City of St. John in the Apocalypse. Yeats imagines he could find in a wine-shop some worker in mosaic who would have the wisdom to answer all his questions. In art, Saints or Angels have the look of "some great bird staring at miracle," almost as if they had achieved *Turīya.* The self is emphasized everywhere, theology with its abstractions has not yet set in: "Could any visionary of those days, passing through the church named with so untheological a grace 'The Holy Wisdom'...fail to recognize some one image seen under his closed eyelids?"[47] Yeats finds an exact parallel between the thought of the Upaniṣads and that permeating Byzantine life.

According to Yeats, the primary and antithetical periods in Christianity flow from Christ's double nature. In himself Christ is antithetical, but in his relationship to mankind, primary. The man in Him, being *antithetical* like His age, knew "intellectual despair" in the Garden. However, that aspect of Christ "which made Christendom was not love," but "*primary* pity, that for the common lot…"[48] While discussing *Turīya* in his introduction to *The Holy Mountain*, Yeats cites the example of Christ. Those who attain seedless *Samādhi* are physically immortal, and like Christ leave an empty tomb and pass into the Source at will. Christ too rose from the dead at a full moon.[49] Yeats finds other parallels:

> When Christ said, 'I and my Father are One,' it is possible to interpret Him as Shri Purohit Swāmi interprets His Master's 'I am Brahma.'[50]

As Yeats grew more confident in his definitions of the two kinds of unity, the primary and the antithetical, he proceeded to re-examine symbolic personages—mythical, literary and living. Persons and characters that had once seemed to exemplify Unity of Being were discovered to be primary; this is the reason why he banished some of them to primary phases. Among those so examined are Christ, Buddha, and Hamlet. His later essays provide much evidence that he learnt through his discussions with Purohit Swāmi that the thought of Buddha was primary, while that of Yājñavalkya and Patanjali was antithetical. Buddha advocated extinction, a total surrender of personality. To Yeats as to the Indians, Buddha represented too great an emphasis on the spirit and a negation of the body, something that could not qualify as Unity of Being. Yeats saw that the philosophy of the Upaniṣads explains in detail both kinds of unity but advocates the antithetical unity symbolized by the full moon:

> The Vedānt philosophers, unlike Buddha, direct our attention to bright or intelligible perfection, but seek timeless perfection, seedless *Samādhi*, beyond it in the isolated Soul, that is yet in all souls.[51]

East and West both have their periods of the bright and dark fortnights, and any nation aspiring for Unity of Being must scrutinize history to discover periods and persons that exemplify this ideal. This is the burden of most of Yeats's later poetry. When Yeats speaks of Greek statues that "put down/All Asiatic vague immensities," and of "the many-headed foam at Salamis,"[52] he is referring to antithetical overcoming primary, but "Asia" is used in a very specific sense. To him, "the East…is not India or China, but the East that has affected

European civilization, Asia Minor, Mesopotamia, Egypt."[53] The latter represents the primary knowledge of dreamless sleep. Examining art to discover philosophy, Yeats finds that geometrical patterns and non-representative art originated in Persia and spread over northern Europe and Asia. Asia here is East, not South. Yeats cites Strzygowski's example of Christ represented by a bare Cross and surrounded by birds, beasts and trees, and agrees that it was created by artists who thought of Him as having no human trait.[54] Looking at modern art Yeats finds in it evidence of a growing primary element in civilization:

> I begin to wonder whether the non-representative art of our own time may not be but a first symptom of our return to the *primary tincture*.[55]

In 'Among School Children' he observed that the children learnt to "be neat in everything/ In the best modern way." Preoccupation with truth as external fact may result in neatness, organization, efficiency, all "modern" virtues, but leaves the soul bankrupt as it were. In 'The Statues' Yeats presents the theme that the ideal of the self in the Upaniṣads was present in Greek civilization as well as in ancient Ireland. Hamlet, "thin from eating flies" represents the empirical self in which an imperfect, incomplete world is constructed out of imperfect data. Reducing the self to the known explains away the reality of a permanent ego. Hamlet represents the modern West characterized by a mainly empirical attitude to reality. "To the empirical individual, if the not-self goes, his individuality also vanishes. So there is a suspicion that the abolition of the objects would reduce the self into a thin abstraction..."[56] The objects of experience require a permanent subject by which they can be experienced. Buddha is contrasted with Hamlet, he is "round and slow...a fat/Dreamer of the Middle Ages..." The self seen as pure subject denies the reality of the content. Therefore, Buddha is a "dreamer." The life without is denied here to save the life within. According to this view, the self is pure subjectivity. Neither the empirical, nor the transcendent view can finally approximate to the self. Yeats marked the following sentence in his copy of *Indian Philosophy* and wrote the word "Ānanda" in the margin:

> Reality is different from thought, and can be reached in the *Turīya* state of highest immediacy which transcends thought and its distinctions, where

> the individual coincides with the central reality.[57]

The *Ātman* is not a pure abstraction, but a fundamental identity of the transcendent and the immanent, which together compose the Absolute. The universal self is both subject and object. Yeats's symbols for this absolute self are Greek statues, perfectly proportioned concrete creations that are the embodiment of perfect ideas; neither "knower" not "known" by itself is of abiding value. "Grimalkin crawls to Buddha's emptiness"; "thin" Hamlet and "fat" Buddha both lack proportion and are far from the unity of a "plummet-measured face."[58]

Whitaker comments that in his later years Yeats would "entirely omit Byzanitum from his panorama."[59] However, when Yeats says in 'The Statues' (written in 1938), "gong and conch declare the hour to bless," he refers to the Hindu and Byzantine ideals of Unity of Being. Earlier, he had informed Sturge Moore that gongs were used in the Byzantine church.[60] So, when he says:

> When gong and conch declare the hour to bless
> Grimalkin crawls to Buddha's emptiness[61]

Yeats expresses his conviction that the ideal of *Turīya* upheld by the Upaniṣads, and the Byzantine ideal of Unity of Being lead to blessedness, whereas Grimalkin and Buddha, with their disproportionate emphasis on mind and spirit respectively, end in "emptiness."

The self is not a void. It is *sat* (truth), *cit* (consciousness), *ānanda* (bliss). Cuchulain is its living embodiment as he is creative joy devoid of fear:

> When Pearse summoned Cuchulain to his side,
> What stalked through the Post Office? What intellect,
> What calculation, number, measurement, replied?

Intellect, calculation, and number are means of understanding the objective world. They cannot be used to understand the subject. In the *Bṛhad-āraṇyaka Upaniṣad* Yājñavalkya tells Gargee: "Do not transgress the limit; or you may go crazy."[62] In other words, intellect cannot comprehend that which is beyond its range. The highest self is the principle of seeing, it cannot be seen; it is the principle of thought, it cannot be defined. Yeats accepts this idea of the self as the underlying unity in all states of consciousness in 'Ribh Considers Christian Love Insufficient':

> What can she take until her Master give!
> Where can she look until He make the show!
> What can she know until He bid her know!
> How can she live till in her blood He live!

The separation of the higher mind from the lower, and the tendency of exalting the lower mind led the modern West to science and its preoccupation with matter. The primary tide that was once pushed back by Phidias had become powerful again in Europe, and Ireland was no exception. Yeats referred to the time when Ireland, inheriting the ideal of unity from Greece, was different from the rest of Europe because her mythology and legends were believed in by noble men and peasants alike, right till the end of the seventeenth century.[63]

This unity of culture had been present in Homer's day, and Yeats advises Irish poets to model themselves on Homer and "reject every folk art that does not go back to Olympus." It was Homer's Greece that symbolized unity as a well-proportioned body, the "plummet-measured face," and not the Greece of Plato; Yeats quoted a contemporary who said: "Greece organized and Greece is dead."[64] After Greece, Byzantium and Renaissance Europe had discovered this Unity for a while.

> Does not one discover in the faces of Madonnas and holy women painted by Raphael or da Vinci, if never before or since, a condition of soul where all is still and finished, all experience wound up upon a bobbin?[65]

Yeats regrets that the unity re-discovered by the Renaissance came to a speedy end. Since both primary and antithetical qualities are visible in the past of Europe, one may select antithetical qualities shared by both Europe and Asia (South) and model oneself upon these. Calculation and number, weight and bulk were of paramount importance to Europe; on the other hand, the magic of *Christabel* or *Kubla Khan* or of Ahasuerus in *Hellas* seemed Asiatic. The presence in its own tradition of these qualities, Europe owed to Asia, Asia here signifying the Far East:

> We have borrowed directly from the East and selected for admiration or repetition everything in our own past that is least European, as though groping backward towards our common mother[66]

for every civilization had begun with Asia. Yeats concludes that a civilization based upon thought cannot be eternal: As he says in 'Meru':

> ...man's life is thought,
> And he, despite his terror, cannot cease
> Ravening through century after century...

Terror of annihilation keeps man searching for the eternal, but the effort of thought to grasp it is futile and comic:

> *And thereupon with aged, high-pitched voice*
> *Aherne laughed, thinking of the man within,*
> *His sleepless candle and laborious pen.*[67]

Thought cannot discover the eternal; it only ends in a negation of itself, "the desolation of reality." In 'Meru' Yeats presents the theme that hermits upon Mount Meru know that man's highest achievements, art, sculpture, and architecture, are physically perishable. Ribh, the Irish hermit, shares this view: "Egypt and Greece good-bye, and good-bye, Rome!" Indian hermits knew that the physical passes away, "before dawn/His glory and his monuments are gone." The Spirit that creates and animates all creation alone endures. In the light of this knowledge, the Indian civilization based itself upon the reality within, the eternal spirit; therefore, it is an eternal civilization. Yeats associates Mount Kailāśa or Meru with *Turīya* or intelligible perfection, and Mount Girnār with *Suṣupti*. He finds that in Ireland, Ben Bulben is the sacred mountain that may be likened to Meru. In 'Under Ben Bulben' he presents the theme that *Turīya*, the unity of being advocated by the Upaniṣads, must be the aim of the Irish poet and sculptor. All the achievements of a civilization are physically perishable, but their value endures eternally if they are generated by the genius that arises in the state of superconsciousness. He gives the example of quattrocento paintings that have a trance like quality:

> Gardens where a soul's at ease;
> Where everything that meets the eye,
> Flowers and grass and cloudless sky,

Resemble forms that are or seem
When sleepers wake and yet still dream,
And when its vanished still declare,
With only bed and bedstead there,
That heavens had opened.[68]

This is unity symbolized by the sacred symbol *aum*, signifying at once immanent and transcendent *Brahman*. Yeats subscribes wholly to the view of the Upaniṣads that the natural and the supernatural are closely blended. According to him, when Europe discovers the antithetical aspect of Christ, it will regain unity, when it finds Him, "not shut off in dead history, but flowing, concrete, phenomenal."[69] Christ, Dante, Blake, and the seers of the Upaniṣads, have all upheld this unity:

> I was born into this faith, have lived in it, and shall die in it; my Christ, a legitimate deduction from the creed of St. Patrick as I think, is that Unity of Being Dante compared to a perfectly proportioned human body, Blake's 'Imagination,' what the Upanishads have named, 'Self.'[70]

Notes

This chapter appeared as my article, 'Yeats's "Unity of Being" in the Perspective of Upanisadic States of *Turīya* and *Suṣupti*,' in *Yeats Eliot Review* (Winter 1994) XII, 81–88.

1 *Vision* (B), p.246.

2 *Holy Mountain*, pp. 36–37.

3 See *Bṛhad-āraṇyaka Upaniṣad*, VI, 2.15–16.

4 *Ibid,* III. 1.6.

5 *Holy Mountain*, p.38.

6 *Ibid,* pp. 22–23.

7 *Māṇḍūkya Upaniṣad*, 12.

8 *Holy Mountain,* p. 29.

9 "Realizing the *Turīya*, the aspirant becomes *Turīya*"; see *The Concept of Ātman*, p. 233.

10 Hume, p.42.

11 See *Essays*, p.518.

12 *Autobiographies*, p.471.

13 See *Essays*, p.245.

14 See *Kaṭha Upaniṣad,* II. 1.1.

15 *Vision* (B), p.88

16 Yeats and Swāmi, p. 149; *Bṛhad-āraṇyaka Upaniṣad*, IV. 3.11.

17 *Vision* (B), p.279.

18 *Patanjali,* p.29.

19 See *Bṛhad-āraṇyaka Upaniṣad*, IV. 4.6.

20 *Holy Mountain*, p.181.

21 (a) Essays, p.483.

(b) A simplistic comparison of *Turīya* and the full moon has led certain critics to see *Turīya* as the second stage(see Introduction, p.16) or to wonder why a being should proceed to the dark moon after attaining enlightenment. Yeats's symbol of the full moon came to stand for the state of enlightenment and unity wherein some impressions remain to be exhausted in future lifetimes, as well as for the final state wherein "all Karma exhausted," the *yogi* achieves entire Unity of Being, becomes *Turīya.*

22 See *Bṛhad-āraṇyaka Upaniṣad,* IV. 4.4.

23 See *Vision* (B), p.135.

24 See *Kaṭha Upaniṣad,* I. 3.3.

25 *Essays*, p. 480.

26 *Bṛhad-āraṇyaka Upaniṣad*, I. 4.10.

27 (a) See *Māṇḍūkya Upaniṣad*, 1. The verse explains that the syllable *aum* is the past, the present and the future, and whatever else there is beyond the threefold time.

(b) Bachchan states in *Yeats and Occultism* that "if he acceptedthe abstract state, proper to the saint, Yeats had to bid farewell to his Muse!" (p.146). He also observes that *Turīya* is the abstract state (p.176). However, Yeats understood *Turīya* exactly. Referring to Vedantic thought he wrote, "this seems to me the simplest and to liberate us from all manner of abstraction and create at once a joyous, artistic life." See *Yeats and Sturge Moore,* p.69

(c) See *Essays*, p.476.

28 *Essays*, p.472.

29 Unpublished letter written on August 27, 1933.

30 *The Later* Phase, p. 261. On 20 September 1933, Yeats stated:

"I think we are speaking of different things. By Unconscious Samādhi I mean *Prayna (Māṇḍūkya Upanishad)* which seems to be interpreted sometimes as 'he who completely knows,' sometimes as 'he who is nearly ignorant' but which according to the translator Dr. E. Roer is used in the *Upanishad* in the first sense. The *Upanishad* says the man in this state 'has become one'—his 'Nature is like bliss.' Later on I find the phrase '*Prayna* (the perfectly wise) who abides in deep sleep.' Sir Arthur Keith speaks of dreamless sleep as a state in which the soul "enters the purest light" and says that in the oldest *Upanishads* only three states of the soul were known. (1) Waking (2) dreaming (3) dreamless sleep. Later a fourth state was added called Turīya, which is a waking state."

31 See *Māṇḍūkya Upaniṣad*, 5.

32 *Indian Philosophy*, I, 160 in Yeats's copy, now in possession of Ms Anne Yeats.

33 See *Essays*, p.476.

34 *Patanjali*, p.32.

35 *Holy Mountain*, p.28.

36 *Vision* (B), p. 82; also see p.183.

37 *Patanjali*, p.35. The spelling of *asamprajñāta* differs, as Purohit Swāmi did not use modern transliteration.

38 See *Vision*, (B) p.183.

39 'The Phases of the Moon,' *Collected Poems*, p.187.

40 *Vision* (B), p. 182.

41 *Concept of Ātman*, p.241.

42 See *Vision* (B), p.258.

43 See Swāmi Nikhilananda, *The Upaniṣads* (London: Phoenix House Ltd., 1954), II, 7: "Objective morality has been relegated to a secondary position in Hindu ethics. If individual perfection is emphasized, so the Hindu philosophers argued, social welfare will follow automatically." (See chapter on 'Hindu Ethics'). Hence cited as Nikhilananda.

44 (a) See *Holy Mountain*, pp.39–40.

(b) Thomas R. Whitaker stated in *Swan and Shadow*, p.22, that "The psychological and religious situation" is mirrored in history, and that "the symbolism derived partly from Blake." Yeats saw that the Upaniṣads define the precise nature of the two states of consciousness, *Turīya* and *Suṣupti*, that he could apply to art and civilization.

45 *Patanjali*, p.15.

46 *Vision* (B), p.274.

47 *Ibid*, p.280.

[48] *Ibid*, p.275.

[49] *Ibid*, p.250.

[50] *Essays*, p.433.

[51] *Holy Mountain,* p.33.

[52] ‘The Statues’, *Collected Poems*, p.375.

[53] *Vision* (B), p.257.

[54] *Ibid*, p.281.

[55] *Ibid*, p.258.

[56] *Indian Philosophy*, I, 161.

[57] *Ibid*, p.165.

[58] See also *Vision* (B), p.71: “pure subjectivity and pure objectivity… are abstractions and figments of the mind.”

[59] See *Swan and Shadow*, p.90.

[60] See *Yeats and Sturge Moore*, p.164. Letter written on 4 October 1930.

[61] For “conch” see Yeats and Swāmi, p.131.

[62] Yeats and Swāmi, p.375.

[63] See *Essays*, p.516.

[64] *Ibid*, p.427.

[65] *Holy Mountain*, p.40.

[66] *Essays*, p.432–433.

[67] ‘The Phases of the Moon,’ *Collected Poems,* p.186.

[68] *Ibid,* ‘Under Ben Bulben,’ p.399.

[69] *Essays*, p.518.

[70] *Ibid*.

Chapter Five

"Imagination," What the Upaniṣads Have Named "Self"

> O sages standing in God's holy fire
> As in the gold mosaic of a wall,
> Come from the holy fire, perne in a gyre,
> And be the singing-masters of my soul.
>
> — 'Sailing to Byzantium'

Art for Yeats was not a means for expression of culture, but a talisman for transforming that culture into Unity of Being. He held the conviction that the arts are inspired by the life beyond the immediate world, and by ancient passions and beliefs. His early ambition was to become "a sage, a magician or a poet."[1] In his *Memoirs* he recorded his wish to receive some "mysterious initiation,"[2] so that he could discover and communicate "a state of being."

He took recourse to many practices that would help him deepen the subjective experience, resulting in revelation. His article, 'Esoteric Spiritualism,'[3] which he wrote as "Fellow of the British Theosophical Society," reveals his desire to communicate with spirits who would impart important secrets to him. He wrote:

> From the *Bhagavad-gītā*, I learn that the one who (in a certain state) is described as the "Lord of all created beings," used this language: "Having command over my nature, I am made manifest by my own power: and as often as there is a decline of virtue, and an insurrection of vice and injustice in the world, I make myself manifest: and thus I appear from age to age." Through thus taking command over his own nature, and all men, I hold that for all practical purposes, he does choose *a chela in human form*: i.e., one who takes on the clothing of *The Sun*... [4]

Yeats inferred that what was true in regard to the Great One, was true in regard to spirits of a lesser degree, who could also have *chelas* or disciples of a degree corresponding with them. Thus Yeats concluded that Vyāsa, the author of the *Mahābhārata* could similarly make himself manifest through a medium. Yeats too wished to receive communication from the adepts of the Orient and asked:

> Will the Brothers of the Orient take to the stripling by recognising him as the "Heir of the Inheritance," and send down a little of the hoarded stores to nurture the new-born life in the valley below?[5]

Yeats was aware of the fact that leading theosophists like Madame Blavatsky and Sinnett were against the practice of invoking the spirits of the dead (see chapter III), and he sought to justify his position in this article. He argued that occultists may regard it wrong to use "controls" to deal with unseen entities and intelligences; in his view, the right or wrong of it depended upon the use that was made of it. He compared the "invocation" of spiritual beings in Indian rituals and ceremonies to the modern practice of séance-holding, and held that increased knowledge and better morals in his age were sufficient justification for engaging in these practices. He expressed his yearning to receive truths from any spirits that might offer to communicate with him:

> Are there not any adept "Brothers" of British or European extraction in sufficient sympathy with the efforts of their own countrymen to open up a direct correspondence with those who are striving to attain a higher order of Life?[6]

One of his objects in joining the Golden Dawn was to practice meditations that would lead to "an evocation of the Supreme Life." As noted by Harper, Yeats was truly devoted to this religious quest.[7] In the essay entitled, 'Is the Order of R.R. and A.C. to remain a Magical Order?' Yeats wrote that he sought "some new descent of the Supreme Life, or may be the presence…of some great Adept, some great teacher."[8]

He went on to study the visions and beliefs of the country people, and to an investigation of contemporary spiritualism, encountering several problems as he proceeded with his practices. In 'Hodos Chameliontos' he discussed the problems regarding communication at séances: were the voices external or internal to the mind? A related question was the mysterious appearance of images in the mind. To what part of the mind did these belong? He asked again: "…from whence came the images of the dream? Not always, I was soon persuaded, from the memory, perhaps never in trance or sleep."[9]

In 1914, Arthur Edward Waite wrote to him that there was little in the Western occult tradition that could throw light on his problem, "though there may be something in the East."[10] Yeats continued to seek answers in a tradition of belief "older than any European Church, and founded upon the experience of the world, before the modern bias."[11] It was this search that led him to study the thoughts of the country people on the one hand, and to an investigation of contemporary spiritualism, on the other.

In his essay, 'Preliminary Examination of the Script of ER,' Yeats was seeking an answer to the question whether the control was a genuine spirit trying to communicate through the medium Elizabeth Radciffe (ER), or a voice, or part of the unconscious memory of the speaker herself.[12] Referring to the 'Script of ER,' he considered that she possibly had access to her own remote memories as well as to the memories of scholars of many languages. Telepathy from scholars' memories seemed a possible explanation. Another question that troubled Yeats was that the impersonal, general mind could reveal its images through the medium and create an illusion of spirit survival: "Is there a world-wide conspiracy of the unconscious mind, of what Maxwell calls 'the impersonal mind' that speaks through dreams to create a false appearance of spiritual intercourse, a seeming proof of the soul's survival after death."[13] It seemed to Yeats that if "the impersonal mind" was a possibility, spirit survival was not; at this stage he did not believe that both could exist simultaneously.

However, he rejected Theodore Flournoy's theory of thought transference, and accepted the view that the controls were independent beings, who knew languages unknown to any person present at the séance.[14] He concluded that spirits were real, not voices in the subconscious mind. Quoting certain unpublished letters of Yeats to Ann Radcliff, G.M. Harper and John S. Kelly point out that he wished "to lay the ghost of any possible form, however mystical, of the subconscious theory," and give her "a refutation of every form of the theory of the unconscious" and in the process discover the means of communication.[15] These excerpts from his letters indicate that Yeats at this time believed that there was only one answer to his questions—

that if voices and spirits were real, there was no such thing as the mystical state in which voices arose from the subconscious mind. These letters were written on 28 July and 17 August 1913, respectively. A passage written in July 1913 in his *Memoirs*, however, indicates that he was privately considering the very possibility that he was seeking to deny in the letters to Ann Radcliff, the possibility, in other words, of the mystical theory. "Having now proved spirit identity—for the ER case is final—I set myself this problem. Why has no sentence of literary or speculative profundity come through any medium in the last fifty years?" He was beginning to distinguish between ordinary communication and poetic inspiration:

> I restate it thus: All messages that come through the senses as distinguished [from] those that come from the apparently free action of the mind—for surely there is poetic inspiration—are imperfect...[16]

He concluded that only practical information "in which the spirits excel us often" could come in through spirits. On the other hand, he noted, "the mind when it seems in contact with their life directly...does not receive messages as to matters of fact." He was thus moving gradually towards a theory that would explain revelation as an inherent power of the mind.

In 'Swedenborg, Mediums, and the Desolate Places' he declared that he had finally learnt of the important distinction between an ordinary medium and a true seer: "He is greatly subject to trance and awakes to remember nothing, whereas the mystic and the saint plead unbroken consciousness." A medium received communication through "extinguishing" his mind while another controlled it (the idea expressed also in the ER script[17]), while the saint and the mystic entered the state of trance consciously and in their waking states.[18] Henceforth, Yeats became more interested in communications from enlightened spirits, and quoted Plutarch as saying that the souls of enlightened men sometimes returned to teach the living. He noted that according to the doctrine of Soho and Holloway, the method of receiving such a communication was not by merely being a passive medium, but by actively seeking higher knowledge: "those studies that have lessened in us the sap of the world may bring to us good, learned, masterful men who return to see their own or some like work carried to a finish."[19]

In 'Anima Mundi' he admitted that the prevailing current theory of forgotten personal memory did not explain things, and accepted Henry More's view that there was a Great Memory passing from one generation to another, containing images which appeared in his mind when he meditated. This explanation, however, was not complete, for it entailed further questions as these images pertained to one's interest, and added to one's knowledge. "If no mind was there…why should I suddenly come upon some detail of cabbalistic symbolism verified at last by a learned scholar from his never published manuscripts…?"[20]

Yeats came close to the view of the Upaniṣads when he considered the possibility that his intensive study had created a link with minds who had followed a like study in some other age. This conclusion confirmed, first, personal immortality, as it indicated the presence of minds of men of another age that were still active, and second, the existence of a Great Memory containing all images out of which they could choose images for communication to the mind of the meditator. This became clearer with his study of the Upaniṣads through which he sought to understand the revelations of *A Vision.* In *A Vision* (1925), in the section entitled 'Mythology,' he stated that "there is a transcendental portion of our being that is timeless and spaceless, and therefore immortal…"[21] According to him, ancient philosophers could prove that even the timeless, spaceless condition of mind is "present vivid experience to some being, and that we could in some degree communicate with this being while still alive, and after our death share in the experience."[22]

It is evident that this comment in *A Vision* was based upon Vedantic studies. Yeats wrote in 'Hodos Chameliontos': "I know now that revelation is from the self, but from that age-long memoried self, that shapes the elaborate shell of the mollusc and the child in the womb, that teaches the birds to make their nest …"[23] He was referring to what is known in the Vedas and Upaniṣads as *Hiraṇyagarbha* (the equivalent of *anima mundi*), a stage in creation wherein are present all the subtle forms of the would-be world. In the phrase "age-long memoried self" Yeats was echoing the *Bṛhad-āraṇyaka Upaniṣad* where the self is spoken of thus: "That self is, indeed *Brahman*, consisting of (or identified with) the understanding, mind, life…"[24] As discussed earlier, the self creates the subtle and gross forms of objects seen by the individual soul in the dreaming and waking states respectively.

Yeats's study of the Upaniṣads taught him that souls which had reached this "timeless, spaceless" state were responsible for the revelations that were received by the seekers and the meditators. The self was the creator of all images in *anima mundi*, the images that appeared to a seer.[25] In a letter to his friend Sturge Moore, Yeats cryptically stated the Vedantic analysis of personality:

> However when one admits, if one does, that mind which creates all is limited from the start by certain possibilities, one admits Platonic ideas, and so a pre-natal division of the 'unconscious' into two forms of mind. This is a Vedantic thought.[26]

In this letter, the Vedantic view of reality is presented by Yeats in a western, analytic, style. In the phrase, "two forms of mind," Yeats refers to the subconscious level that contains all images and ideas, and also to the state beyond this, which is referred to by the Upaniṣads as the *Ātman* or pure-consciousness, devoid of mind. This is the consciousness without content reached by the seer, which Yeats, in the absence of suitable western terminology, christens as a "form" of the unconscious mind. Yeats explained in his essay on the *Māṇḍūkya Upaniṣad* that the westerners called the self "the unconscious" because of their analytic attitude: "because we sit in the stalls and watch the play....The Indian, upon the other hand, calls it the conscious, because, whereas we are fragmentary, forgetting, remembering, sleeping, waking, spread out into past, present, future, permitting to our leg, to our finger, to our intestines, partly or completely separate consciousness, it is the 'unbroken consciousness of the Self,' the Self that never sleeps..."[27]

An understanding of the four states of the soul as described in the Upaniṣads, finally provided the answer regarding dream images, psychic phenomena, and revelations from spirits. (Yeats noted in 'Anima Mundi' that he saw no reason to distinguish between mental images and apparitions.) He described the four states as symbolized by the mystic word AUM thus:

> 'A' is the physical or waking state; 'U' the dream state, where only mental substances appear; 'M' is deep sleep, where man 'feels no desire, creates no dream,' yet is this sleep called 'conscious' because he is now united to sleepless Self, creator of all....The Self, whereto man is now united, expressed by our articulation of the whole word, is the fourth state.[28]

He also referred to these states in *A Vision* (1937), and quoted lines about the dream state from the *Bṛhad-āraṇyaka Upaniṣad.*[29] The passage about the dream state marked in his copy of R.E. Hume's *Thirteen Principal Upanishads* is as follows:

> There are no chariots there, no spans, no roads. But he projects from himself chariots, spans, roads. There are no blisses there, no pleasures, no delights. But he projects from himself blisses, pleasures, delights. There are no tanks there, no lotus-pools, no streams. But he projects from himself tanks, lotus-pools, streams. For he is a creator.[30]

The last sentence, it is important to note, is underlined by Yeats. He had understood and noted the view of the Upaniṣads, that it is the immortal spirit of man that both creates and sees these dreams. This view explained not merely that dreams were evidence of an abstract Great Memory or *anima mundi*, but also that *anima mundi* itself was the creation of the Supreme Self which was variously described as "Emperor," "the Immortal," and "the Golden Person" in the Upaniṣads.[31] In 'Byzantium' Yeats speaks of the Supreme Self that ever creates new images:

> The golden smithies of the Emperor!
> ...
> Those images that yet
> Fresh images beget.

This analysis of the four states of the soul also enabled him to divide the communicating spirits into two categories:

> Those who inhabit the "unconscious mind" are complement or opposite of that mind's consciousness and are there, unless as messengers of the *Thirteenth Cone*, because of spiritual affinity or bonds created during past lives.[32]

It is obvious here that the spirits associated with a person through bonds in past lives belonged to one category. These were the "unpurified dead" that appeared in dreams. These spirits were really ghosts and belonged to the dream state of the Upaniṣads and to the *Passionate Body* of Yeats's system in *A Vision*. They could appear in the séance room and give information that had only personal relevance.

To the other category belonged "those in freedom through contemplation" that Yeats termed messengers of the Thirteenth Cone;

these brought about not mere information but revelation of truth. As stated above, Yeats felt that meditation upon certain matters seemed to have put him in touch with those who had mastered similar themes in previous ages; this idea was corroborated by the Upaniṣads. In 'A General Introduction For My Work' he quoted a verse from the *Chāndogya Upaniṣad*: "A wise man seeks in Self, those that are alive and those that are dead and gets what the world cannot give."[33] Truth was to be gained not so much through communication with spirits at a séance, as through meditation upon the self. *Svetāśvatara Upaniṣad* advocates a meditation on spiritual teachers:

> To one who has the highest devotion (*bhakti*) for God,
> And for his spiritual teacher (*guru*) even as for God,
> To him these matters which have been declared
> Become manifest [if he be] a Great soul (*mahātman*)[34]

It was this experience of grace that Yeats prayed for in 'Sailing to Byzantium':

> O sages standing in God's holy fire
> As in the gold mosaic of a wall,
> Come from the holy fire, perne in a gyre,
> And be the singing-masters of my soul.

Such spirits belong to the eschatological state called *Purification* described in 'The Soul in Judgment' in *A Vision*, and are therefore seen as standing in "a holy fire." Yeats says the memory of such spirits is so completely obliterated that they remember not even their names; they are at last completely free, and associate with other free spirits. In the *Bṛhad-āraṇyaka Upaniṣad*, Yājñavalkya explains to his wife Maitri that in the state of freedom, particular consciousness is no more.[35] According to Yeats, such spirits may choose to communicate truths because the purification requires the completion of some "synthesis" left unfinished in their past incarnation. They appear to those who share with them "some affinity of aim." Yeats found out why the instructors had revealed to him the system of *A Vision*. They taught him the system, not for his sake, but their own. These pure spirits, having lost individual consciousness, act in groups. Yeats remembered that a spirit once said to him: "We do nothing singly, every act is done by a number at the same instant," and concluded that perfection implied a shared purpose or idea.[36] Yeats discovered the same idea in the Upaniṣads. He noted in his introduction to *The Holy Mountain* that having reached enlightenment, a man was no longer alone: "He was not isolated, however, as are men of genius or intellect, for henceforth all those in whom that Self had awakened were his neighbours."[37] All liberated spirits came together into a unity. He added in his essay on the *Māṇḍūkya Upaniṣad* that

> in so far as *Satva* reflects the Self, it is common to all whose minds contain the same reflection: the images of the Gods can pass from mind to mind, our closed eyes may look upon a world shared, as the physical world is shared, though difference in the degree of purity has been substituted for difference of place.[38]

In this Self, in other words, "all delivered selves are present." He mentioned the same idea in his introduction to *Aphorisms of Yoga* translated and edited by Purohit Swāmi.[39]

He realized that a study of the Upaniṣads was relevant to psychical research. He wrote in his Preface to *The Ten Principal Upanishads*:

> Psychical research, which must some day deeply concern religious philosophy, for its evidences surround the pilgrim and the devotee though they never take the centre of the stage, has already proved the existence of faculties that would, combined into one man, make of that man a miracle-working Yogi. More and more too does it seem to approach a main thought of the Upanishads.[40]

According to Yeats, the view of the Continental investigators comes very close to the thought of the Upaniṣads on this subject, as they too present an individual self possessed of power and knowledge; they are not very far from defining it as the Self of all, wherein they can seek the living and the dead. Yeats noted that the thought of the Upaniṣads offered perhaps the only explanation that could reconcile the two explanations offered by Continental and American investigators regarding psychic phenomena:

> In England and America it is attributed to spirits, whereas almost without exception, Continental investigators discover its origin in some hitherto unimagined power of the individual mind and body. These points of view, spiritism and animism, are not in the eyes of the student of Yôga contradictory; to quote the *Chāndôgya-Upanishad*, 'the wise man sees in Self those that are alive and those that are dead.'[41]

It is important to consider the relevance of Yeats's questions and experiments regarding the nature of the mind, to his poetry. Examined in the light of the Upanisadic division of the states of consciousness into waking, dreaming, deep sleep, and absolute consciousness, Yeats's poetry is seen becoming more and more complex as it arises out of progressively deeper levels of consciousness.

During the early period, he was increasingly aware that the reason for the weakness of his poetry was his preoccupation with purely individualistic desires and dreams. For instance, 'The Lake Isle of Innisfree' was composed in a mood of homesickness; it was a poem that he did not think much of, later.[42] He also grew critical of an early play, *The Land of Heart's Desire,* for its exaggerated sentimentality. He wrote to George Russell about it: "The popularity of the 'Land of Heart's Desire' seems to me to come not from its merits but because of this weakness. I have been fighting the prevalent decadence for years, and have but just got it under foot in my own heart."[43] This decadence resulted when a poet created only from one part of his mind, a fraction of his total experience, and put his "vague desires into his art..." Yeats shared responsibility with the Rhymers for the prevailing decadence in lyric verse, and in *The Tragic Generation* he analysed it as being due to their insistence upon emotion which had no relation to any public interest. Upon re-reading his early poems he found them full of "romantic convention, unconscious drama."[44]

The other cause of weakness of his early plays and poems was the predominance of abstraction and philosophy, which had not been transmuted into art. His plays, *Where There is Nothing,* and its later version, *The Unicorn from the Stars,* are weak because they are merely debates between abstract theories of life; between a view of life as organised, lawful work, versus one that upholds a life of trance, contemplation, and general inaction. He gradually realized that philosophy must be totally embodied in character and action, and gave the example of *The Countess Cathleen:* the play began as the moral question regarding a soul sacrificing itself for a good end, but gradually philosophy was eliminated till all ideas were transmuted into dialogue. What he said of George Russell and his religious group was true of his own early plays: "One of their errors was to continually mistake a philosophical idea for a spiritual experience."[45]

He began to pray that his imagination might somehow be rescued from abstraction, and become as engaged with life as Chaucer's imagination had been. He was also able to put his finger on the real reason for the sentimentality of his verse: it was his refusal to permit it any share of an intellect which he considered impure. By abstraction he meant "not the distinction but the isolation of occupation, or class or faculty;"[46] in other words, emotion, and hope, as well as thought must find their synthesis in poetry.

His experiments with evocation through symbols revealed to him a deeper level of consciousness. The discovery of *anima mundi*, the storehouse of racial memory, made possible poems like 'The Second Coming' and 'A Prayer for My Daughter.' He wrote: "The Second Coming! Hardly are those words out/When a vast image out of *Spiritus Mundi*/Troubles my sight…"A poet who could "see" the images in the memory of the race or the *anima mundi* had entered the subconscious mind of the race.

From a decadent poet who merely composed verse expressing his personal desires and wishes, Yeats became a poet-sage who spoke on behalf of this one mind. He wrote:

> I have always sought to bring my mind close to the mind of Indian and Japanese poets, old women in Connacht, mediums in Soho, lay brothers whom I imagine dreaming in some medieval monastery the dreams of their village, learned authors who refer all to antiquity; to immerse it in the general mind where that mind is scarce separable from what we have begun to call 'the subconscious'…[47]

The philosophy of the Upaniṣads, he found, corroborated this view. The letter to Sturge Moore mentioned earlier is significant as it shows the relationship between Vedantic thought and Yeats's poetic theory and practice. Of Vedantic thought he said, "This seems to me the simplest and to liberate us from all manner of abstraction and create at once a joyous, artistic life."[48] This meant that the poet must turn inwards and give expression to the highest experience of his own race; in order to do so it was necessary to move away from the waking state, the conscious mind.

Yeats's speculations on spiritism were also the result of his desire to understand the nature of poetic inspiration. He wrote in his *Memoirs* that messages did not come only through submerging one's conscious will, "for surely there's poetic inspiration," but also from what could be called "free action of the mind."[49] In the second version of *A Vision* he substituted for *anima mundi* the term *Celestial Body*, for whereas the former was racial memory, and was seen from the point of view of the individual, the latter was seen as a part of the larger unity—it was one of the *Principles* created by the Absolute. It was not memory in itself but was responsible for it. When Yeats asked his instructors, "whose perception then do we share?" He was told that it was not a remembered perception, and was left to find an answer.[50] This answer he found in the concept of *Hiraṇyagarbha*, to which he referred in *A Vision* as "the divine ideas in their unity." The perfection arrived at by the spirit in the state called the *Purification*, was embodied in one of several attitudes. Thus the *Celestial Body* contained those ideals that could find embodiment in human life. The poet could aid the process by interpreting and copying them in his poetry and drama. As Yeats explained:

> The *Spirit's* aim, however, appears before it as a form of perfection, for during the *Purification* those forms copied in the arts and sciences are present as the *Celestial Body*... I connect them in my imagination with an early conviction of mine, that the creative power of the lyric poet depends upon his accepting some one of a few traditional attitudes, lover, sage, hero, scorner of life. They bring us back to the spiritual norm.[51]

For the poet who would seek to know the ideas in the *Celestial Body*, it was important to communicate with superior spirits who possessed this knowledge. Yeats felt that a really great work resulted when the poet discovered some knowledge that came to him from beyond his mind. He was convinced that an artist could become a tool in the hands of superior powers who gave him images he could not have chosen himself.[52] He admitted that his poetry "gained in self-possession and power" owing to the incredible experience of communicating with instructors who gave him metaphors for poetry. The system of symbolism that revealed itself was completely strange to him and his wife. The fact that there was similarity between his own themes in *A Vision* and those of Spengler indicated to him that he had finally touched the one mind.[53] Spengler had referred to "whole metaphors and symbols that had seemed my work alone." This was exhilarating as Yeats had in any case not sought originality of thought, but the most fundamental thought. Originality that amounted to narrow individuality, had resulted in decadence. In 'Anima Mundi' he had written, "it is not permitted to a man who takes up pen or chisel, to seek originality, for passion in his only business..."[54] A poet was a part of a community of spirits, a "phantasmagoria." As Yeats wrote in 'A General Introduction For My Work':

> Talk to me of originality and I will turn on you with rage. I am a crowd, I am lonely man, I am nothing. Ancient salt is best packing.[55]

These spirits helped to enhance his knowledge of human nature that he had presented in *Per Amica Silentia Lunae*.[56] They made him realize the view of the Upaniṣads that meditation upon a particular problem brings help from supernatural agencies or enlightened spirits, as mind enters a state where it is one with them. This idea of the Upaniṣads was understood and explained by A E. Referring to him Yeats wrote:

> A poet, he contends, does not transmute into song what he has learned in experience. He reverses the order and says that the poet first imagines and that later the imagination attracts its affinities.[57]

Yeats expressed the same view in 'The Tower':

> ...being dead, we rise,
> Dream and so create
> Translunar Paradise.

His prolonged researches into spiritism, and his desire to make poetry out of the highest experience of man, amounted to meditation and brought about revelation. That he also actually meditated he recorded in *A Vision*:

> At Oxford I went constantly to All Souls Chapel, though never at service time, and parts of *A Vision* were thought out there...and once I remember saying to a friend as we came out of Sant' Ambrogio at Milan, "That is my tradition and I will let no priest rob me."[58]

His notion of poetic creation conformed in essence to that presented in the Upaniṣads. In fact, the Upaniṣads have a single word for the Creator, the sage and the poet: *Kavi*, a word which is etymological shorthand for "one who has intuitive wisdom," or "one who creates and sees images."[59] According to the Upaniṣads, the poet partakes of the creative power of the One mind, the power that Yeats referred to as "Blake's 'Imagination,' what the Upanishads have named 'Self.'"[60]

Notes

1 *Autobiographies*, p.64.

2 *Memoirs,* p.36.

3 This article is reprinted in a collection of writings by T.S. Subba Row, *Esoteric Writings* (Adyar: The Theosophical Publishing House, 1895, rpt. 1931), pp. 201–215. The original publication details are not available, but it must have been written in 1888 when Yeats became a member of the Theosophical Society, or in 1889 when he joined the Esoteric Section of the Society.'

4 (a) *Ibid.,* p.202.

(b) The quotation from the *Bhagavad-Gītā* is from IV. 6, 7.

5 *Ibid.*, p.207.

6 *Ibid.*, pp.214–215.

7 See *Golden Dawn*, p.74.

8 *Ibid,* Appendix K.

9 *Autobiographies*, p.261.

10 See *Letters to Yeats*, p.279; A.E. Waite wrote:

"So far as my studies can tell you, the theory of Astral Light as a receptacle of forms, and having therefore "pictures" therein was first originated by Eliphas Levi after the year 1860…It has been said to be in Jacob Boehme, but this is untrue also. Finally it is not in Paracelsus…I would help you if I could over this side of the question, but it is one for a reliable eastern student, on the understanding that he is not a theosophist."

11 *Autobiographies*, p.265.

12 See 'Preliminary Examination of the Script of ER' in *Yeats and the Occult*, p.143.

13 *Ibid.*, p.144.

14 *Ibid.*, p.151: "My theories changed continually [constantly] until I got what I believe to be clear evidence that 'the controls' know

languages unknown to any person present...This case would be accounted for by Flournoy by thought transference, but I do not think anybody has suggested that you can account for answers in a tongue unknown to all present by thought transference from a distant [absent] person."

15 *Ibid.*, p.135. According to Harper and Kelly, Yeats came to the conclusion in the ER script that the long dead communicate with the recently dead.

16 *Memoirs*, p.266.

17 See *Yeats and the Occult*, p.156: "It is plain that the muscles of her hand can record what her mind's eye sees without the conscious control of the intellect...She is really automatic in certain states...."

18 (a) See *Explorations,* p.50.

(b) *Memoirs*, p.266: "By medium I mean spirit impulse which is independent of, or has submerged, the medium's conscious will."

19 *Explorations*, p.60.

20 *Mythologies*, p.345.

21 *Vision* (A), p.251.

22 *Ibid.*, p.252.

23 *Autobiographies*, p.272.

24 *Bṛhad-āraṇyaka Upaniṣad*, IV. 4.5.

25 See *Vision* (A), p.250: "the seer amidst brilliant light discovers myths and symbols that can only be verified by prolonged research. He has escaped from the individual *Record* to that of the race."

26 *Yeats and Sturge Moore*, p.69.

27 (a) *Essays*, p.480.

(b) Leo, the control who communicated with Yeats as his " anti-self," had also referred to this state: "when the animal spirits withdrew from the man in trance or in death, this (*spiritus mundi)* formed his airy body, and was…plastic." He stated it was what in "error, your century has named the unconscious." Leo quoted by Arnold Goldman in 'Yeats, Spiritualism and Psychical Research,' *Yeats and the Occult*, p.119.

28 *Essays*, p.476.

29 See *Vision* (B), p.220.

30 (a) Hume, p.134.

(b) In the Vedas and Upaniṣads various terms are used to designate the creative power or the imagination of the Creator, e.g., *kāma, tapas, īkṣaṇa or māyā.*

31 (a) See *Bṛhad-āraṇyaka Upaniṣad*, IV. 3.12, 13.

(b) "The Golden Person" is *Hiraṇyagarbha*, containing "name and form" in its womb.

32 *Vision* (B), p.237.

33 *Essays*, p.509. Yeats is referring to *Chāndogya Upaniṣad*, VIII. 3.2. Also see Yeats and Swāmi, p.109.

34 Hume, p.411; *Svetāśvatara Upaniṣad*, VI. 23.

35 (a) See *Bṛhad-āraṇyaka Upaniṣad*, II. 4.12–14.

(b) Also see Śaṁkara's comment in Nikhilananda,. III, 182:

"No more is there such a thought as: 'I, So-and-so, am the son of So-and-so; this is my land and wealth; I am happy or miserable.' For such particular consciousness is due to ignorance, and since ignorance is absolutely destroyed by the realization of Brahman, how can the knower of Brahman, who is established in his nature of Pure Intelligence, possibly have any particular consciousness?"

36 *Vision* (B), p.234.

37 *Holy Mountain*, p.17.

38 *Essays,* p.482.

39 (a) See *Patanjali*, p.15: "Matter, or the soul's relation to time has disappeared; souls that have found like freedom in the remote past, or will find it in the future, enter into it or are entered by it at will..."

(b) Yeats found the same idea in Christian mysticism: "reality itself is found by the Daimon in what they call, in commemoration of the Third Person of the Trinity, the Ghostly Self. The blessed spirits must be sought within the self which is common to all." *Vision* (B), p.22.

40 Yeats and Swāmi, p.9.

41 (a) *Patanjali,* p.21.

(b) Aksakoff had distinguished between different mediumistic phenomena in his book *Animismus and Spiritismus (*Leipzig, 1890). This is cited in Leslie Shepard, ed. *Encyclopedia of Occultism and Parapsychology* (Detroit: Gale Research Company, 1984), I, 15.

42 Yeats wrote to Ruth Watt in 1929: "Please don't think 'The Lake Isle of Innisfree' is better than all the other poems, for I don't." Yeats Ms. 5918, National Library of Ireland.

43 *Letters*, p.433; written in April, 1904.

44 *Autobiographies,* p.103.

45 *Ibid.*, p.467.

46 *Ibid.,* p.190.

47 *Mythologies,* p.343.

48 *Yeats and Sturge Moore*, p.69.

49 *Memoirs*, p.266.

50 See *Explorations*, p.331.

51 *Vision* (B), p.234.

52 See *Autobiographies*, p.272.

53 (a) See *Yeats and Sturge Moore*, p.105.

(b) See *Vision* (B), p.18. Also, "Certainly my instructors have chosen a theme that has deeply stirred men's minds though the newspapers are silent about it." *Ibid.*, p.262.

54 *Mythologies*, p.339.

55 *Essays*, p.522.

56 See *Vision* (B), p.9. Yeats noted that his instructor had taken his theme from his recently published *Per Amica Silentia Lunae*; Browning's Paracelsus experienced revelation after writing his spiritual history, and Wilhelm Meister read his own history written by another before he became an initiate.

57 *Essays,* p.416.

58 *Vision* (B), p.6.

59 See *Īśa Upaniṣad*, 8. Radhakrishnan refers to Śaṁkara's explanation of *kaviḥ* as *krānta-darśi* or seer, one who has intuitive wisdom. See *The Principal Upaniṣads,* p. 573.

60 *Essays*, p.518.

Chapter Six

Yeats's Theory of Symbolism in the Light of the Upaniṣads

> Pythagoras planned it. Why did the people stare?
> His numbers, though they moved or seemed to move
> In marble or in bronze, lacked character.
> But boys and girls, pale from the imagined love
> Of solitary beds, knew what they were...
>
> — 'The Statues'

As we have seen in the previous chapter, Yeats's lifelong preoccupation was to write poetry based on truths perceived in moments of revelation, "to discover and communicate a state of being."[1] Of the two, the first, "to discover," related to the domain of the mystic, the second, "to communicate" was the responsibility of the poet. Yeats soon discovered that the latter was indeed a difficult task. He noted in his *Memoirs* a saying of Mohini Chatterjee: "I thought truth was something that could be conveyed from one man's mind to another's. I now know that it is a state of mind."[2] Mohini Chatterjee's philosophy was derived from the Vedas and the Upaniṣads. It held that the highest truth was beyond the intellect and really a state of mind. The *Ṛg Veda* explained that the seeker after truth becomes the ultimate reality himself; his individuality is lost and no objectivity remains outside him.[3] So what and to whom should he communicate? The *Bṛhad-āraṇyaka Upaniṣad* also voiced the view that communication presupposes the duality of subject and object, but where everything becomes one's own self, and all duality vanishes, communication becomes impossible.[4] Yeats quoted Coventry Patmore who held that religious truth could not be taught to another, only a way could be pointed out by which he might find it for himself.[5] Yeats came to see the truth of this idea through his personal experience; he found that it was difficult to communicate all that he had experienced in the state of trance. He recorded his inability to describe some vision to Lady Gregory, and remembered that sometimes lecturers on mysticism had to stop in the middle of a sentence.[6]

Another aspect of the difficulty was that although one could articulate what one had experienced, one could not communicate entirely, as the giver and the recipient lacked the common ground of experience; while writing his essay on 'Magic,' he tore up many pages describing incidents that would seem meaningless and obscure to the reader. Many a time he had wished to speak of the strange images that had risen in the deeps of his mind, but had decided against it.[7] He was convinced that where there was no common ground of belief, there could be only disbelief and ridicule, and concluded that any effort at communication should be aimed at protecting believers, rather than convincing the sceptics.[8]

However, as a seer-poet, Yeats realized that he was different from a magician who kept the secrets of his vision to himself. He must convey to the best of his ability, his experience and knowledge, as he held an idealistic view of art and poetry. "Imagination is always seeking to remake the world according to the impulses and patterns in the Great Mind,"[9] he said, and the poet was an instrument of that mind. If his art was pure, and free from "heterogeneous knowledge and irrelevant analysis," the artist became a medium for the creative power of God.

Yeats spoke in 'The Symbolism of Poetry' of his passionate belief that the arts would cure "the slow dying of men's hearts," without necessarily using religious and theological language, as the latter was ceasing to attract the modern man. The eternal, essentially incommunicable state of being, had to be evoked in men's minds; spiritual truths had to be restated in a language that was poetical and literary. The poets had long used myths and symbols for the purpose of communicating to the people esoteric truths, in an exoteric form.

According to Harper, Yeats was inspired most consistently by Blake's aesthetic doctrine that the seer must communicate visions through symbol.[10] However, in his essay on 'Magic,' Yeats admitted reading "some Indian book," as well as Blake, on the subject.[11] His belief in the power of symbols had an occult basis also in theosophical writings, which derived their authority largely from the Upaniṣads. The *Bṛhad-āraṇyaka Upaniṣad* held that the self was endowed with desire, was, in other words, the power that could create objective phenomena.[12] This idea had been amply explained in theosophical publications; an article on 'Thoughts on the Metaphysics of Theosophy' referred to the fact that it was possible to modify circumstances and control the elements by their intellectual powers, "which are other and more intensified forms of the will."[13] Yeats expressed his belief that "the gross is the shadow of the subtle" in 'The Symbolism of Poetry.' In this essay he elaborated on the view that seemingly feeble things had been proved to possess overwhelming power at times.

This was an important law that Yeats observed, and applied to occult as well as poetic practices. For instance, it was a firm faith in the principle that imagination could create circumstance that enabled him to oppose confidently the formation of secret groups inside the Order of the Golden Dawn. According to him, this formation of groups would evoke distrust among members and lead to disruption: "such an obsession even if it had not supported the real disorders I have described, would have created, so perfectly do the barriers of conscious life copy of the barriers of the superconscious, illusionary suspicion…" He was always to maintain that:

> The central principle of all Magic of power is that everything we formulate in the imagination, if we formulate it strongly enough, realizes itself in the circumstances of life…[14]

Harper comments that here Yeats was not in agreement with the other members, as he insisted on upholding his "personal philosophy and aesthetic" regarding magic. "Magic, as he uses the term, is a means of breaking down the barriers between the phenomenal or conscious world and the spiritual or superconscious world."[15] However, Yeats's "personal philosophy" was based on the above mentioned law, also upheld by Madame Blavatsky, that "when a thought of good or evil import is begotten in our brain, it draws to it impulses of like nature as irresistibly as the magnet attracts iron filings."[16]

Yeats realized that the writer or artist could creatively exploit this law, in order to impress his ideas upon an age. Madame Blavatsky had clarified, that it was due to the "thought impulse" making itself "felt in the ether," that it was possible that "one man may impress himself upon his own epoch so forcibly that the influence may be carried...from one succeeding age to another until it affects a large portion of mankind."[17] One way of effecting this change was through understanding the "mystical value of human language." A priest or an occult magician could bring about a certain effect in the objective universe with the help of symbols and incantations. Madame Blavatsky admired the practice of this law by ancient Indians:

> Nowhere is the mystical value of human language and its effects on human action so perfectly understood as in India, nor any better explained than by the authors of the oldest *Brahmanas*....The greatest power of this *vach*, or sacred speech, is developed according to the form which is given to the Mantra by the officiating Hotri...If pronounced slowly and in a certain rhythm, one effect is produced; if quickly and with another rhythm, there is a different result.[18]

Yeats asserted the truth of this principle in his magical practices; in 'A Postscript to Essay called "Is the Order of R.R. and A.C. to remain a Magical Order?"' he said: "It is a first principle of our illumination that symbols and formulae are powers, which act in their own right and with little consideration for our intentions, however excellent. Most of us have seen some ceremony produce an altogether unintended result because of the accidental use of some wrong formula or symbol."[19] Evidently, Yeats applied to his experiments in the Golden Dawn, theories he had learnt through theosophy.

Like the magician, the poet too could, with the help of symbols, rhythm, and metre, affect the minds of men. According to Yeats, an emotion, in order to become effective, had to be expressed in colour or in sound or in form; these, in different modulations and arrangements would evoke different emotions; thus poets and painters were constantly affecting mankind. He said again, "Have not poetry and music arisen, as it seems, out of the sounds the enchanters made to help their imagination to enchant, to charm, to bind with a spell themselves and the passers-by?"[20]

In Indian thought he found not only a corroboration, but progressively a clearer exposition of the philosophical and psychological principles that underlay symbolism. He expressed in his essay on 'Magic' his three convictions: first, that the borders of our mind were ever shifting, so many minds would flow into one another to create a single mind; second, that the borders of our memories were also shifting, so that our memories became a part of the great memory of Nature herself; third, that this great mind and great memory could be evoked by symbols.[21]

In the background of these convictions was the Vedic view of creation. As discussed in the chapter on "Nature," reality is seen as four successive stages of existence, of which manifestation is the fourth and final stage. The first stage is that of the formless absolute, indiscrete, indescribable.[22] The next stage is that of the First Cause that has the potential to create, pregnant with the concept of "I." In the third stage, this Creator becomes charged with desires, ideas or notions, which are the seeds of the tangible world; the fourth stage is the tangible world of multiformity. By a process of passing through these stages the formless assumes form; according to this philosophy, the created universe is His symbolic representation which suggests His existence.[23] 'One' is therefore at the root of the many, a natural corollary being that this very process must repeat itself in all aspects of the resulting creation. Thus man becomes the microcosmic reflection of the macrocosmic reality. In man too, there are these four stages,[24] though the process of realization moves in a reverse direction. To the immediately perceptible, tangible world, corresponds the waking stage, in which the senses and the mind operate. To the state pervaded with ideas and notions, corresponds the dreaming stage in which the mind sees its own desires or images of objects seen in waking life. The third stage is known as deep sleep, or *Suṣupti*, in which the objects and their images go dormant, to come into operation again in the dreaming or waking states. The final stage, corresponding to the formless absolute, is *Turīya* in which the I-consciousness of the third stage is transcended, and there is only pure consciousness.

The seers of the Upaniṣads based their spiritual practices upon this philosophy of the macrocosm and the microcosm. If the universe was a symbol of the Creator and finally of the formless Absolute, by meditating upon an object chosen from it one could finally reach the reality at its base. So they devised the method of meditation upon symbol, a method in which waking, dream and dreamless sleep became stages in meditation, finally leading to merger with the Absolute.

That Yeats understood much of this philosophy is clear from his writings. His three convictions enumerated above indicate that he was unaware of the first stage, that of the formless Absolute, but understood quite well the relation between the one mind, its ideas, memories and images. This was familiar to him as *anima mundi*, and later as *Celestial Body* or *Hiraṇyagarbha.* The process through which he learnt of these stages is discussed in the chapter on "Imagination." Just as in religious meditation one begins with a familiar object, and passes through various stages to understand and be at one with the Creator, similarly a work of art must be pondered over, its meaning understood, and its experience shared. So creation and meditation are two complementary activities: the poet expresses his unique experience through symbols whereby the reader understands him.

This basic philosophy with its attendant ramifications offers a complete explanation of Yeats's theory of symbolism. In his essay on 'Magic,' he speaks of the one mind and one memory shared by people at some deep, subconscious level. In the *Ṛg Veda* and the Upaniṣads, ultimate reality is seen as intelligence, *mānas*, or the supreme mind, which pervades the regions of nature as well as the heart of man.[25] Sometimes, in the dream state, an individual may see visions or images of the ideas in the mind of the Creator. It is also by virtue of the One having become many, that many may share these visions. Yeats verified some of this philosophy with the help of experiments conducted in the Golden Dawn, and concluded that the same vision may appear to several people; he also recorded a particular instance of one dream shared by three people.[26]

According to the Upaniṣads, objects or events experienced in the waking state leave their impressions on the mind. We have seen in the chapter on "Death and Immortality" that although an experience passes away, its "husk" or image remains in the mind. The memory of a vital experience of joy or sorrow is preserved in the mind of an individual over several lifetimes, and very often reappears in some other shape in the dream state, to fructify at some future period. The *Bṛhad-āraṇyaka Upaniṣad* has it that in the dream state, the self remains awake and notices the impressions of the deeds.[27] This indicates that the human mind has an inherent power to reduce to an image or impression, an event of the past, and to foresee through an image, an event in the future; this impression or image is the symbolic form of that experience or event. The *Praśna Upaniṣad* explains that in dream or in vision a seer may come in contact with the images preserved in the memory or the racial record:

> There in sleep, that god (mind), experiences greatness. He sees again whatever object has been seen, he hears again whatever has been heard, he experiences again and again whatever has been experienced in different places and directions....what is existent and what is non-existent, he sees all; being all he sees (all).[28]

The verse indicates not only that in dreams there are reproductions of waking experiences, but also that sometimes there are new constructions. Yeats discovered that the mind can reproduce in a changed form, the experiences of waking life. He narrated that when he dreamt in words, he knew his father to be tall and bearded; if, however, he dreamt in images, he sometimes discovered him represented by a stool or the eye-piece of a telescope.[29] From this he concluded that we cast off the "concrete memory" but not the "abstract memory" when we sleep. Thus abstract memory may be said to be symbolic of the original experience. This led him to realize that the mind itself is nature's own workshop of symbols, a view that he would find corroborated by the Upaniṣads. The self is immortal and contains the memory of Nature, hence events may be seen in symbolic form either during the same lifetime, or in subsequent lifetimes.

Basing his theory on the view of the Upaniṣads, Yeats's friend A E traced the process by which the mind transmuted a historical event or legend, into symbol:

> These dreams, antiquities, traditions, once actual, living, and historical, have passed from the world of sense into the world of memory and thought...from things which the eye can see and the ear can hear, they have become what the heart ponders over...and are...more suitable for literary use, than the day they were begotten. They have now the character of symbol, and as symbol are more potent than history.[30]

Yeats also said in 'Magic,' that whatever had attracted the passions of man over generations became a symbol in the "Great Memory," and could be used by one who had mastered the secret, to arouse powerful emotions. In other words, imitating nature, a poet too can compress an experience into a symbol, and evoke through it his own experience in the mind of the reader, as far as it is possible. Experience, when shaped into symbol, becomes an inherent part of it. Thus a symbol carries a particular meaning right from inception and concentration on symbol ultimately unfolds it. According to Yeats, magicians, using this principle, consciously created and used symbols, poets and other artists using them half unconsciously. For a poet they were the only effective means of communication: "I love symbolism, which is often the only fitting speech for some mystery of disembodied life..."[31]

Armed with this philosophy, Yeats successfully countered the criticism of his contemporary, John Eglinton, who advocated that writers discontinue the use of ancient legends as these "refuse to be taken up out of their old environment and be transported into the world of modern sympathies."[32] Yeats argued that John Eglinton preferred a poetry that was, "like all the lusts of the market place, 'an expression of the age' and of 'the facts of life.'" Yeats asserted his own belief in poetry that renewed an interest in ancient, universal belief, "old faiths, myths, dreams."[33] A E in "Literary Ideals in Ireland," said defending Yeats, that the inherent power of myths and symbols was due, not only to the fact that they were a part of the great memory shared by a people, but also to their embodying universal truths:

> I think that the tales which have been preserved for a hundred generations in the hearts of the people must have had such a power, because they had in them, a core of eternal truth.[34]

Yeats, like the seers of Upaniṣads, realized that the mind was not a closed, separate entity. He contrasted the modern tendency to praise the individual life with the view of the ancients who were always praising the one mind.[35] It was because the power of a symbolic poem depended upon a common memory, a shared ground of belief, that Yeats always sought symbols that were familiar, concrete, and had some link in the memory of the race. It must be clarified here that whereas he was eclectic in his search for ancient thought, ranging over Eastern and Western philosophy alike, he insisted on drawing his symbols from his race and nationality. Thought must be as close to eternal truth as possible, and must be communicated:

> Supreme art is a traditional statement of certain heroic and religious truths, passed on from age to age, modified by individual genius, but never abandoned.[36]

However, as different races gave a different expression, a different embodiment to eternal truths, the poet too must draw symbols from his own race; he strongly disapproved of the practice of picking up stories and symbols from everywhere. "Have not all races had their first unity from a mythology that marries them to rock and hill?"[37]

It was a cardinal tenet of Yeats's theory of symbolism that symbols must be rooted in time and space, in history and geography alike. To illustrate how symbolism worked, he cited the example of the Indian *yogi* who must fix his eye and thought upon the point of his tongue which symbolized all the senses. "He must not meditate upon abstractions, nor, because unseen, upon eye and ear."[38] He spent some time marking in red ink upon a large map every sacred mountain. Also, some communication was instantaneous if the reader focused his attention on the known. "The distant in time and space," he wrote, "live only in the near and present."[39] The reason why he was critical of Shelley, was that the latter often chose unfamiliar symbols. In 'Art and Ideas,' Yeats spoke of the richness that was lost to Shelley's *Prometheus Unbound* because he had not discovered his Caucasus in England or in Ireland. Yeats instructed Sturge Moore that the tower he was to draw should resemble the real object, and added: "I like to think of that building as a permanent symbol of my work plainly visible to the passer-by."[40]

The entire burden and aim of Yeats's art was to create unity, to re-create the one mind that Europe had been and had ceased to be. He observed that this idea, for long a mere opinion of his, had finally turned into a firm conviction:

> Nations, races, and individual men are unified by an image, or bundle of related images, symbolical or evocative of the state of mind which is, of all states of mind not impossible, the most difficult to that man, race or nation.[41]

This "state of mind" that he sought to convey was the "Self" of the Upaniṣads, Blake's "Imagination" and Dante's well-proportioned body, or "Unity of Being." Yeats was, however, clearly aware that the mystic state, being an indescribable experience, would result in obscurity in his poetry.

Keeping in mind the principle that symbols must be drawn from one's own race, he tried to evoke unity of being through several symbols drawn from western history and geography. The chief among these was Byzantium as pictured in the two poems, 'Sailing to

Byzantium' and 'Byzantium.' Yeats consciously used Byzantium, a physical entity, a city, a period rooted in space and time, as a symbol of *Turīya*, a timeless state. What happens to the mystic in *Turīya* took place in Byzantium too. The physical was transmuted into a symbol of the immanent spirit, "those walls with their little glimmering cubes of blue and green and gold,"[42] and the drilled pupil of the eye underwent a somnambulistic change. Thus Yeats superbly put into practice his theories of art discussed at great length in 'Magic,' and in 'The Symbolism of Poetry.' In the two Byzantium poems he created a symbol to evoke images buried in the memory of the race; he attempted binding with a spell his own mind, when he would enchant the mind of others, in order to create "the seeming transitory mind made out of many minds." He had, it is obvious, created a symbolic talisman of the sort medieval magicians made, attempting to capture, in complex colours and forms, "a part of the Divine Essence." He demonstrated that just as a state of mind can expand into history (an idea discussed in the chapter on "Unity of Being," and also acknowledged by Whitaker[43]), history too can contract into a state of mind, thus becoming symbol.

The self, according to the Upaniṣads, is not to be attained through the effort of the intellect or through pursuit of objects in the external world. The Old Man in *At the Hawk's Well* voices this view:

> And do you think so great a gift is found
> By no more toil than spreading out a sail,
> And climbing a steep hill?[44]

In this play Yeats pictured man's search for the hidden self in terms of specifically Irish figures and setting; the self is personified in the Woman of the Sidhe who is "bird, woman or witch,"and Cuchulain is the hero who seeks her as his immortal self.[45] In 'The Statues' Yeats again presents the Irish hero Cuchulain as a symbol of the highest reality that cannot be defined through the empiric means of "calculation, number, measurement." Yeats always sought to identify his beliefs with his country: in plays like *The Words Upon the Window Pane, Purgatory,* and *The Herne's Egg*, he presented in terms of Irish setting and characters, truths about fate and destiny, eschatology and immortality, that he learnt substantially from the Upaniṣads.

Another tenet of Yeats's symbolism was that experience must be linked to geographical reality. Ancient memories could be better revived if evoked by Slieve-na-mon or Croagh Patrick. After reading about Bhagwān Shri Hamsa's experience on Mount Kailaśa, Yeats wrote: "We have learnt from Dante to imagine our Eden, or Earthly Paradise, upon a mountain, penitential rings upon the slope."[46] He noted in his introduction to *An Indian Monk* that Purohit Swāmi's experience was similar to the experience of European mystics. In 'Under Ben Bulben' he gave it geographical reality through the symbol of Ben Bulben, the Irish mountain, and described it thus:

> And when its vanished still declare,
> With only bed and bedstead there,
> That heavens had opened.

Racial symbols, according to Yeats, were important as a means of attaining the experience of the ultimate. He asked Purohit Swāmi if a European, undertaking a similar journey, would have shared the experience of Bhagwān Shri Hamsa. Upon getting a negative answer, he concluded that Shri Hamsa's experience of revelation "depended in part upon innumerable associations from childhood on, in part upon race memory." Yeats knew that Mount Kailaśa was a symbol of some "act of creation" in the racial memory of the Aryans.[47]

However, Yeats became aware through the revelations of his instructors in *A Vision*, and through his study of the Upaniṣads, that symbols drawn from nature, sun, moon, and sea for example, were universal, shared by West and East alike. The bright fortnight, leading to *Turīya* in the Upaniṣads, is paralleled by the full moon in European symbolism. Europeans would see the waxing moon as representing man's personality as it developed and moved to perfection at the full moon. These symbols have been discussed in the chapter on "Unity of Being"; Yeats noted that the European symbol of the full moon corresponded to the symbol of the sun in the Upaniṣads; the underlying concept, he saw, was the same.

Another symbol that Yeats regarded as universal, was that of lake or sea as a symbol of the mind of man. The Upaniṣads speak of the world of generation as a sea;[48] Yeats speaks of this sea in 'Sailing to Byzantium.' He also noted that lake Mānas Sarowar meant "The great intellectual lake." When he describes the sea near Rapallo, "houses mirrored in an almost motionless sea," he seems to give it the same symbolic significance. The symbol of the road or path in the Upaniṣads is also used by him. *The Bṛhad-āraṇyaka Upaniṣad*, for example, speaks of "the narrow ancient path which stretches far away, has been touched (found) by me, has been realized by me."[49] Yeats echoes the same idea and symbol when he speaks of the mountain road from Rapallo to Zoagli as illustrating something he had discovered in his own mind.[50] He uses the symbol again in 'Lapis Lazuli,' in the picture of the "lofty slope" and the "little half way house/Those chinamen climb towards..." In each case the road symbolizes the effort of man to disentangle himself from the mundane and the temporal, and progress towards his inner spirituality.

However, all symbols, whether local, historical, or universal, are only of secondary, not primary importance. The levels of meaning and experience must be progressively reached by the reader. The efficacious symbol is one in which the reader has some idea of the meaning associated with it, and intended by the writer (otherwise, as Yeats had noted in 'Magic,' two confusing pictures would rise in the mind). Historical events, for instance, could function as symbol only if the right areas were meditated upon. As Yeats noted, belief in the Incarnation invoked modern science and modern efficiency; "the historical truth of the Incarnation is indifferent, though the belief in that truth was essential to the power of invocation."[51] In the practice of symbolism, meditation must be accompanied by concentration on the meaning of the symbol. This explains the relation of Yeats's prose work, his essays and introductions, his vast correspondence, even of the two versions of *A Vision*, to his poetry. The prose works expound, as far as it is possible to do so, the meaning of his work, while the poems and plays encompass it and seek to evoke the experience that is beyond the meaning. Commenting on Yeats's style in *A Vision*, Whitaker has said that "Yeats's historical sympathies are not simple...his prose is constantly shaped by the power of ironic qualifications."[52] Keeping in mind both the poetic and prose descriptions of say, Byzantium, it is obvious that in the poems history has been transformed into symbol through a process of selection and emphasis. However, looking only at the prose, one is led to ask the question, why the "ironic qualifications?" Yeats was not writing history with its scrupulous emphasis on fact. In his prose he was differentiating between those aspects of Byzantine history which represented unity, from those which represented abstraction, in order to enable the reader to understand the poems. He was indicating that the reader must select the areas representing unity, and associate them in his mind with the symbol offered in the Byzantium poems.

In the final stage, symbol and meaning alike give way to experience, which is of ultimate importance: "another turn of the gyre and myth is wisdom, pride, discipline."[53] In terms of the *Principles*, symbolism is the *Celestial Body*, the cloak that must be discarded that spirit be revealed, as he explains in 'The Soul in Judgment,' section VII. The symbol itself vanishes in giving birth to experience. This aspect is illustrated in the case of Bhagwān Shri Hamsa who said that when the mental image of the God vanished, he had the transcendental experience of *Turīya*.[54] It was in order to learn about the state ensuing symbolic worship, that Yeats urged Purohit Swāmi to write about his experience, as he noted in his introduction to *An Indian Monk*.

A symbol thus led one to "the near and yet hidden"; it was important in so far as it facilitated "a return to the sources of our power."[55] This idea became the theme of his poem, 'A Dialogue of Self and Soul':

> That flowering, silken, old embroidery, torn
> From some court-lady's dress and round
> The wooden scabbard bound and wound,
> Can, tattered, still protect, faded adorn.

The heroic tales and mythologies, "old embroidery" on silken cloth, that formed the tradition of a race may have become so old and faded that few understood their meaning, yet were important as they had protected or enshrined the eternal spirit, the "consecrated blade" that is "unspotted by the centuries." Tradition was precious if it performed its function of symbol leading a people to a realization of the spirit: "nor is mythology mere ostentation... if it draws me onward to the unknown."[56] Tradition must be used to "follow to its source/ Every event in action or in thought..." This results in the bliss evoked by the childlike and joyous rhythm of the closing lines of the poem: "We must laugh and we must sing,/We are blest by everything,/ Everything we look upon is blest."

However, the experience of bliss reached, spirit flows back into the body. The experience of *Turīya* best explains the relationship between body and soul, symbol and experience. As Yeats says, those who have attained this experience are said to be physically immortal, although invisible. They leave, like Christ, an empty tomb and pass into the Source.[57] In other words the symbol, the physical aspect, is not altogether discarded, it is transformed into the likeness of spirit. A reader's progress from symbol to final experience has four stages corresponding to the states of waking, dream, dreamless sleep, and pure or absolute consciousness. The first stage is that of the concrete symbol, the second that of identity between concept and image, or theme and symbol. In the third state there is only this identity; here the meaning may be understood as far as possible. As Yeats explains in his introduction to *The Māṇḍūkya Upaniṣad*, the third state of meditation is in form, that is, meaning is still linked to symbol and through it to the racial comprehension of the final experience. In the fourth state pure meaning, bereft even of racial interpretation, gains supremacy. Yeats noted the difference between the third and fourth stages in the case of the spiritual experience of Bhagwān Shri Hamsa:

> The Mantra, the sacred fire that he must presently light, the caress given to all parts of his body, are from the memory of the race, the immemorial ritual; but 'the initiation into the realization of the Self' is wordless, unique, an act of unbroken consciousness alone.[58]

The experience is "wordless" because (as discussed earlier in this chapter) it is an experience in which subject and object become fused. As the *Bṛhad-āraṇyaka Upaniṣad* asks, who should communicate and to whom?

It is to be remembered, however, that even through symbols communication or evocation is partial; symbolic poems cannot be deciphered like allegory; the latter, Yeats said quoting Blake, is formed by the "daughters of memory."[59] It is supremely important that the reader be close to the experiential level of the writer. This is why communication of poetic experience must remain partial, only those aspects of it capable of being evoked in the reader's mind, which the latter has himself experienced. The same idea can be understood in terms of Yeats's *Principles*. *Spirit* is pure mind that contains pure truth; this *Spirit* is the Daimon's knowledge. It is *Mānas* or the great mind containing all knowledge, and *Creative Mind* containing all the universals, is a faculty of the *Spirit*. The proportion of the whole that man possesses consciously is symbolized by a particular phase of the moon. Similarly the *Mask* represents the mind's growth in self-knowledge (in one lifetime or several), symbolized by the waxing moon, till, at last, this knowledge complete, man becomes capable of sharing the experience of the poet. Only those who have reached this state understand and share the experience compressed in a symbolic poem, more especially if it is an experience of a mystical state. The essential idea is that only when an experience is common to reader and poet, is communication absolute, complete. Such a reader is a rarity. Yeats writes:

> A hundred generations might write out what seemed the meaning of the one, and they would write different meanings, for no symbol tells all its meaning to any generation... [60]

In 'Ireland and the Arts,' Yeats dealt at great length with the relative importance of communication and artistic merit in a great work. He felt strongly that an artist's true business was not to aim at popularity, but to please himself; he quoted Walt Whitman:

> The oration is to the orator, the acting is to the actor and actress, not to the audience:
>
> And no man understands any greatness or goodness, but his own or the indication of his own.[61]

In the same essay he also quoted Edwin Ellis, who said that it was not the business of the poet to make himself understood, but the business of the reader to understand him. And he wrote to Sturge Moore in 1926 that he did not care to "prove" his special experiences to "the majority of teachers in universities...What matters to me is that it is my experience."[62]

Yeats summed up in 'The Statues' the reaction of those in whose minds he had not evoked this experience. In the line, "why did the people stare?" he indicated that it was a "stare" of incomprehension on the part of those who looked for "character," for certain definable qualities in art which they could grasp at once. On the other hand, "boys and girls, pale from the imagined love/ Of solitary beds, knew what they were"; these boys and girls represented persons who shared the poet's experience. They found in art a concrete embodiment of what they "imagined" but could not express, so their response was one of spontaneous rapport— they "pressed at midnight in some public place/Live lips upon a plummet-measured face."

According to the Upaniṣads, all knowledge is contained in the mind and may be retrieved through meditation.[63] Yeats shared this view and applied it to poetry, believing that a great symbolic work of art demanded deep and prolonged meditation. He explained in 'Symbolism in Painting' that it was the artistic counterpart of the talisman made by mediaeval magicians; it required to be pondered over. Yeats's view was that the purpose of both art and religion was to attain the "Divine Essence"; the method remained the same regardless of whether a religious or an artistic symbol was used, for ultimate reality was one.[64] Through the method of meditation it was possible to cross the conscious mind and reach the unconscious mind. This could bring about not only knowledge, a change in the brain, but a transformation of one's whole life, because what the *Spirit* knew became a part of itself; he had explained this in 'The Completed Symbol' in *A Vision*. In his early years, Yeats had spoken to the members of the Golden Dawn of this change wrought by meditation:

> The more vigorously they evoke the White Light in their recurrent meditation, the more active will their personal life become, the more decisively will it diverge from the general life, the more perfectly will it realize its isolated destiny.[65]

Yeats discovered the underlying principle in the story of the courtesan who had prayed, "not foreseeing its consequence, not only for physical, but for spiritual health, and the 'unconscious mind' had heard her prayer."[66]

It is possible to conclude that for Yeats symbolism was not "mere ostentation," but a fuller statement of the function of poetry. This function was identical to the function of religion: to awaken the divine life in the unconscious mind, or in the words of his poem 'Sailing to Byzantium,' "to keep a drowsy Emperor awake," and thereby transform one's entire life. If this effort of the poet could be shared by his readers, an entire nation, or even civilization, could be exalted into a state of spiritual wholeness or unity of being.

Notes

1 *Memoirs*, p.42 .

2 *Ibid.*, p.145.

3 See *Ṛg. Veda,* X. 82.7.

4 See *Bṛhad-āraṇyaka Upaniṣad*, IV.5.15.

5 See *Memoirs*, p.170.

6 *Ibid.,* p.128.

7 See *Essays,* pp.37–38.

8 *Ibid.*, p.38.

9 *Ibid.*, p.52.

10 See *Golden Dawn*, p.104.

11 (a) See *Essays*, p.46.

(b) Yeats wrote to Ernest Boyd in 1915: "My interest in mystic symbolism did not come from Arthur Symons or any other contemporary writer…Of the French symbolists I have never had any detailed or accurate knowledge." *Letters*, p.592.

12 See *Bṛhad-āraṇyaka Upaniṣad,* IV. 4.5.

13 (a) Sandaram Iyer, "Thoughts on the Metaphysics of Theosophy," *Theosophical Miscellanies* No. 1. (1883).

(b) Madame Blavatsky too, in *Isis Unveiled*, had said that every objective manifestation required will and force, and these three were convertible forces. *Isis*, I, 198.

14 "Is the Order of R.R. and A.C. to remain a Magical Order?" *Golden Dawn*, p.265.

15 *Ibid.*, p.55.

16 *Isis*, I, 181.

17 *Ibid.*

18 *Ibid.*, II, 409.

[19] *Golden Dawn*, p.269.

[20] *Essays*, p.43.

[21] *Ibid.*, p.28.

[22] See *Ṛg. Veda* X, 129, 2–3.

[23] (a) See Swāmi Ms., 'Philosophy of the Upanishads': "That Being is the seed, all else is His expression."

(b) See Usha Grover, *Symbolism in the Āraṇyakas and their Impact on the Upaniṣads* (New Delhi: Guruvar Publications, 1987), p.8.

[24] See *Māṇḍūkya Upaniṣad*, 2–7.

[25] See *Concept of Ātman*, p.270. "This One intelligence appears variously as perception, thought, impulse, memory"; *Aitareya Upaniṣad* cited in *Concept of Ātman*, p.110.

[26] See *Essays*, p.33; *Memoirs*, p.183.

[27] See *Bṛhad-āraṇyaka Upaniṣad*, IV. 3.11.

[28] *Praśna Upaniṣad*, IV. 5.

[29] (a) See *A Vision* (B), p.229.

(b) "Our dreams select for their purpose images that may go extra-ordinarily close to those of memory, but never coincide with them." *Letters*, p.708.

[30] AE in *Literary Ideals in Ireland* (London: T. Fisher Unwin, 1889), p.50. Hence cited as *Literary Ideals.* This work is a compilation of articles that appeared in the Saturday issues of the *Daily Express*, Dublin. According to the editor, "they constitute a controversy which was not intended when the first article was written, but which spontaneously grew from week to week." Those who participated in the controversy were W.B. Yeats, AE, John Eglinton, and W. Larminie.

[31] *Essays*, p.382.

[32] John Eglinton, "Mr. Yeats and Popular Poetry," *Literary Ideals*, p.41.

33 *Ibid.*, W.B. Yeats, "John Eglinton & Spiritual Art," p.36.

34 *Ibid.,* AE, "Literary Ideals in Ireland," p.50.

35 (a) See *Essays*, p.44.

(b) See 'A Postscript to Essay called "Is the order of R.R. and A.C. to remain a Magical Order?"' *Golden Dawn*, p.270: "individuality is not as important as our age has imagined."

36 *Autobiographies*, p.490.

37 *Ibid.,* p.194.

38 *Ibid.*, p.441.

39 *Ibid.*

40 *Yeats and Sturge Moore*, p.114.

41 *Autobiographies,* p.194.

42 *Vision* (B), p.281.

43 See *Swan and Shadow*, p.22. See chapter IV, "Unity of Being", note 44 (b).

44 *Collected Plays*, p. 212.

45 *Ibid.*, p. 216.

46 *Holy Mountain*, p.20.

47 See *Essays,* p.485.

48 See *Kaṭha Upaniṣad*, I. 3.2; *Praśna Upaniṣad*, VI. 8.

49 *Bṛhad-ārṇyaka Upaniṣad*, IV. 4.8.

50 See *Vision* (B), p.7.

51 *Autobiographies*, p.482.

52 *Swan and Shadow*, p.88.

53 *Explorations*, p.345.

54 See *Holy Mountain,* pp.178-181/*Essays,* pp.477-479.

55 *Explorations*, p.345.

[56] *Ibid.*

[57] See *Essays*, p.465.

[58] *Ibid.*, p.480.

[59] *Ibid.*, p.382; see also pp.146-147.

[60] *Ibid.*, p.148.

[61] *Ibid.*, p.207.

[62] *Yeats and Sturge Moore*, p.99.

[63] See *Muṇḍaka Upaniṣad*, II. 2.3.

[64] See *Essays*, p.207.

[65] See *Golden Dawn*, Appendix K, p.264.

[66] *Essays*, p.450.

Conclusion

Yeats's achievement as a modern interpreter of the Upaniṣads is that he combines experiment with faith, a scientific curiosity with a regard for ancient wisdom. As he wrote in his introduction to *The Holy Mountain*: "We prove what we must and accept the rest upon hearsay."[1] The tradition of occult experiment that existed in ancient India before the doctrines were finally formulated in the Upaniṣads is now lost. It must be acknowledged that Yeats in his own way, through experiment and séance, experience, meditation, and trance, sought to confirm the truths of the Upaniṣads. His detailed and lifelong study of occult laws was part of his keen desire to understand intellectually what he believed intuitively. His very method was Upanisadic in character, that is, he relied not upon a single faculty but upon a combination of all faculties. He wrote:

> I do not think I have been easily convinced, for I know we make a false beauty by a denial of ugliness and that if we deny the causes of doubt we make a false faith, and that we must excite the whole being into activity if we would offer to God what is, it may be, the one thing germane to the matter, a consenting of all our faculties.[2]

The Upaniṣads did not offer dogma but truths that could be explained or understood intellectually. Yeats acknowledged that in the Western tradition "fragments of belief" existed but the "explanatory intellect had disappeared."[3] In the Upaniṣads he found "an ancient discipline, a philosophy that satisfied the intellect."[4] Living in a scientific age, he realized that these doctrines would have no appeal to his readers, unless proved or presented rationally.

According to the Upaniṣads, the world is a manifestation of the idea of the Creator; this view Yeats accepted, as he saw that an evolutionist philosophy (such as he found in Plotinus and the neo-Platonists), by separating spirit from matter, culminated in a materialistic view of nature. He held the view instead that "Natural and supernatural with self-same ring are wed."[5] The physical aspect of life, or the beauty of nature was not rejected by the Upaniṣads, where the Supreme was both immanent and transcendent. Yeats found in this philosophy an alliance between body and soul not accepted by orthodox Christian theology; the Upanisadic view supported his own basic convictions.

The doctrines of the Upaniṣads threw a great deal of light on the strange symbolism of *A Vision*. Yeats understood that it is due to innate ignorance that ultimate reality, the sphere, appears divided into the antinomies of subject and object, time and space. Failure to see the underlying unity impels man to seek without what lies within. This philosophy with its belief in rebirth explained the symbolism of the phases of the moon in *A Vision*, where Yeats depicted how man moves from phase to phase, as he chases mask after changing mask in pursuit of happiness.

One of the problems that troubled Yeats was the nature of revelation. There was no evidence of profound truths coming through spirits at séances, yet his personal experience of voices or "instructors" revealing truths, indicated that inspiration was a fact of the higher spiritual life. American and European spiritualists held contradictory views on revelation. The former generally held spirits responsible for it, while the latter maintained that it was an inherent power of the mind. Yeats found that Upanisadic thought not only reconciled the two views, but also explained the matter in a clearer light. According to the Upaniṣads, in the state ensuing deep and prolonged meditation, the mind ceases to be a closed, personal entity, and the person enters into communion with kindred spirits who complement its knowledge, or impart the knowledge he seeks.

Yeats also found that his occult experiments regarding the nature of the mind yielded certain basic laws that were supported by the Upaniṣads. For instance, the Upanisadic doctrine that imagination was a power of the mind, that could turn thought or emotion into circumstance, became the basis of his mature poetic practices. By meditating upon unity of being, and then creating poems in which this experience was embodied with the help of symbols, he wished to imprint this unity on an entire race or nation.

The thoughts of the Upaniṣads became the cornerstones of Yeats's belief. He embodied them in innumerable poems and plays using Christian and Irish symbols that would be familiar to his readers. His desire to help Shree Purohit Swāmi in translating the principal Upaniṣads, also stemmed from his wish to spread their thoughts in simple English. A study of this monumental translation is instructive not only for the Orientalist, but also for a reader of Yeats's poetry. To the latter it offers important insights, leading to a better understanding of Yeats's later poems and plays.

Reviewing Yeats's attempt to introduce an "alien" tradition into the West, H.R. Bachchan says: "Yeats found a 'system' from which to draw inspiration for his poetry, but he failed to provide one that could be accepted as a tradition."[6] Yeats wrote that he and his contemporaries, when they were young, "talked much of tradition" and men like Francis Thompson, Lionel Johnson and others found it in Christianity. But *The Golden Bough* had made Christianity look "modern and fragmentary."[7] We understand Yeats's fascination for the Upaniṣads when we realize that he was trying to rediscover and reaffirm the truths upon which a common human tradition is based. As he wrote in his introduction to *The Holy Mountain*: "No two civilizations prove or assume the same things, but behind both hides the unchanging experience of simple men and women."[8] This unchanging experience, common to Western and Eastern folk alike, was Yeats's subject. He realized that if he was to be a seer as well as a poet, and move men's minds, he must trace tradition back to its source:

> I am content to follow to its source
> Every event in action or in thought...[9]

If tradition was in history and time, its "source" lay in the timeless. He said that like T.S. Eliot, he found in Christianity "a convenient symbolism" for ancient or newer thought.[10]

Yeats's understanding of the Upanisadic concepts of *Suṣupti* and *Turīya* helped him in clearly defining his views on the relation between life and art. Mastery of the meaning of art can take the reader only as far as the state of *Suṣupti* (dreamless sleep), the realm of "name and form," in the words of the Upaniṣads. Definitions of *Suṣupti* by Yeats and Purohit Swāmi employ the image of the statue, and are an indication that art in itself is not an end. However idealistic the image presented in art, this image is only a medium for inspiring life. In the 'The Statues,' Yeats gives two graphic examples of this conviction: Phidias's art "Gave women dreams and dreams their looking glass"; the young press "Live lips" upon a "plummet measured face."[11] Art is therefore a mirror of the higher life, by contemplating which "the man within" must shape himself. It is a medium for rejuvenating life, not merely an object for "staring" at, for objective, critical analysis. It is important that the highest experience possible to man be part of the poet's vision. Art must bring about *Turīya*, the unified consciousness in the waking state. This had been Yeats's highest aspiration as a poet-seer. He had written to Ethel Mannin of his wish to make "a last song, sweet and exultant, a sort of European *geeta*, or rather my *geeta*, not doctrine but song."[12] As he put it in the last days of his life: "When I try to put it all into a phrase I say, 'Man can embody truth but he cannot know it.' I must embody it in the completion of my life."[13] His achievement may be summed up in Purohit Swāmi's words to him:

> They say that East and West 'shall never meet,' but forget history.... it is only in the Spirit that there has been, or can be meeting. You had vision, you saw truth; you proclaimed it.[14]

Notes

[1] *Essays*, p.448.

[2] *Explorations,* p.31.

[3] *Essays*, p.429.

[4] *Ibid.*

[5] *Collected Poems*, p.328.

[6] *Yeats and Occultism*, p.270.

[7] Yeats and Swāmi, p.10.

[8] *Holy Mountain*, p.11.

[9] *Collected Poems*, p.267.

[10] Yeats and Swāmi, p.10.

[11] *Collected Poems*, p.375.

[12] *Letters*, p.836.

[13] *Ibid.*, p.922. Letter written on 4 January 1939.

[14] Purohit Swāmi, trans. *The Geeta: The Gospel of the Lord Shri Krishna* (London: Faber and Faber Ltd., 1935), Swāmi's dedication to Yeats.

Appendix

Septenary Division in Different Indian Systems*

We give below in a tabular form the classifications adopted by the Buddhist and Vedāntic teachers, of the principles of man:

Classification in *Esoteric Buddhism*	Vedāntic Classification	Classification in Tāraka Rāja-Yoga
1. Sthūla-śārira	Annamaya Kośa*	Sthūlopadhi.$ (1–3)
2. Prāna.+	Prānamaya Kośa. (2–3)	
3. The vehicle of Prāna#		
4. Kāma Rūpa	Manomaya Kośa. (4–5a)	
5. Mind (a) Volitions and feelings etc.		Sūkshmopādhi. (5a–5b)
5. Mind (b) Vijñāna	Vijñānamaya Kośa.	
6. Spiritual Soul.	Ānandamaya Kośa.	Kāranopādhi.
7. Ātman.	Ātman.	Ātman.

* Kośa (Kosha) is "sheath" literally, the sheath of every principle.

\+ "Life."

\# The astral body or Linga-Śārīra.

$ Sthūla-Upādhi, or basis of the principle. Buddhi.

* Reproduced from H.P. Blavatsky, *The Secret Doctrine* (Madras: The Theosophical Publishing House, 1978), I, p. 157.

Index

D

Daimon,the, 56, 57, 62, 81, 83, 84, 86, 90, 94, 157
Dante, 108, 121, 152
Dark moon, the, 15, 105, 106, 115
Destiny, 57, 60, 82, 92

E

Ellmann,Richard, 12
Yeats: The Man and the Masks, 3, 18
Eliot, T.S., 166

F

Fate, 90, 91, 92
Four Faculties, the, 12, 14, 56–57, 59, 63, 108, 113
Four Principles,the, 12, 47, 48 54–57, 59, 63, 81–83, 93, 94, 108, 157
Fraser, G.S., 15, 17
Full moon, the, 15, 16, 17, 105, 106, 108, 154

G

Golden Dawn, The, 4, 5, 17, 76, 77, 127, 146, 147, 149, 159
Gonne, Maud, 77
Gregory, Lady, 79
Visions and Beliefs in the West of Ireland, 6, 7, 76–78, 83, 145
Grimalkin, 118

H

Hamsa, Bhagawān Shri, 3, 106, 109, 154, 156, 157
The Holy Mountain, Yeats's introduction, 3 15, 16, 80, 93, 105–107, 112, 116, 134, 164, 166
Hamlet, 14, 96, 97, 116–118
Harper, G.M.,
Yeats and the Occult, 2, 18, 128
Yeats's Golden Dawn, 2, 4, 5, 17, 127, 145
Hegde, Narayan, 3, 16
Hermetic Society, the, 5
Hiraṇyagarbha, 19, 48–49, 53, 130, 137, 149
Horton,William, 1
Hough, Graham,
The Mystery Religion of W.B. Yeats, 1, 4, 11
Hume, R. E., 7, 10, 28, 35, 83
The Thirteen Principal Upanishads, 10, 85, 107, 132

I

Irish Theosophist, The, 46
Īśvara (Supreme Being), 48, 53

J

Johnston, Charles, 3, 7
From the Upanishads, 45, 46, 78

W

Y

Irish Studies

Edited by Robert Mahony

The popularity of Irish Studies among both students and scholars has grown very markedly in the 1980s and 1990s, extending well beyond Ireland. This series is designed to serve and foster that interest. Currently featuring works in Irish history and literature, this interdisciplinary series will broaden its scholarly range in the future to include political and cultural studies generally.

For further information, or the submission of manuscripts, please contact:

Peter Lang Publishing
Acquisitions Department
275 7th Avenue, 28th Floor
New York, New York 10001